PRAISE FOR *BREAKING OLD RHYTHMS*

"Sculpting and painting words into eloquent and raw poetry seems to be the breath of Amena Brown. *Breaking Old Rhythms* is a call for all who find themselves stuck in the mundane, drawing us to risk, push and open our full potential—all the while realizing we have been and always will be completely seen and completely loved by the One who started the creating."

LISA GUNGOR, singer-songwriter

"Through her beautiful style and thoughtful expression, Amena Brown artfully fractured my structured rhythm to challenge me to consider a new perspective of God's work in my life and faith."

JENNI CATRON, executive director of Cross Point Church and coauthor of *Just Lead!*

AMENA BROWN

FOREWORD BY DAN KIMBALL

BREAKING OLD RHYTHMS

ANSWERING
THE CALL OF
A CREATIVE GOD

IVP Books

An imprint of InterVarsity Press
Downers Grove, Illinois

InterVarsity Press
P.O. Box 1400, Downers Grove, IL 60515-1426
World Wide Web: www.ivpress.com
E-mail: email@ivpress.com

While all stories in this book are true, some names and identifying information in this book have been changed to protect the privacy of the individuals involved.

Cover design: Cindy Kiple
Interior design: Beth Hagenberg
Images: modern dancer: ©jonya/iStockphoto
textured background: ©Hedda Gjerpen/iStockphoto

ISBN 978-0-8308-4301-5

Printed in the United States of America ∞

Library of Congress Cataloging-in-Publication Data
A catalog record for this book is available from the Library of Congress.

P	18	17	16	15	14	13	12	11	10	9	8	7	6	5	4	3	2	1
Y	28	27	26	25	24	23	22	21	20	19	18	17	16	15	14	13

DEDICATION

To Jesus,
the DJ of all DJs,
the Greatest Master of Ceremonies,
the Ultimate Teacher of the break dance.
You create and break my rhythm, and I'm always better for it.

CONTENTS

FOREWORD

*I*magine that you have had the experience when a song gets stuck in your head and you just can't get it out. You find the song popping up in your mind throughout the day. You tap the beat with a pen. You hum the tune. This isn't necessarily a bad thing when the song is respectable. But more often than not, it seems, it happens with a song you wouldn't normally want to be associated with.

For me, usually the song is new, overproduced teen pop, with a chorus that has a super catchy hook to it. I'd never, ever listen to it on my own, but when I hear it suddenly on the radio, it just annoyingly sticks right in my head. Then during the day, over and over I think of the song and rhythm, and without even realizing it I sing a line or two of the chorus as I walk down a hallway. I end up sitting at my desk humming and tapping away to the rhythm and beat of the song until someone hears me and walks away thinking I am into teen pop music.

Undesirable, annoying and embarrassing songs and rhythms can get stuck in our heads, but they generally fade out of our minds after a day or two. But what about when the thing that is stuck in your head isn't just a teen pop song but the way you are living your life? You are repeating a cycle; you instinctively know there is something different for you, but you don't know how to break out of the rhythm you are in.

If you've felt or experienced this, you're not alone. There are so many of us who have felt stuck in a rhythm of life that we wish we weren't in, that we wish we could change. The good news is that we can break out of those rhythms. God is bigger than any rhythm we get ourselves into.

I can't think of anyone better to help us understand how God can break us out of old rhythms into new ones than my friend Amena Brown. I remember meeting Amena for the first time several years ago when we were both speaking at a conference for young leaders. Amena got on the stage and began reciting Scripture. But her Scripture reciting was done in the poetic form of spoken word. I was absolutely mesmerized by it. I have heard Scripture read many times, but this was the first time hearing it with such raw emotion—emotion that felt totally connected to the passage being read. I couldn't wait to hear her each time she took the stage; her poetry and readings were quite honestly the highlight of the whole event. Amena spoke in rhythms, and these rhythms were infused with God's truth.

What you will appreciate about this book is that Amena fuses God's truth with the reality of the rhythms of life. In *Breaking Old Rhythms* you will not read Christian lingo or get an unrealistic, over the top, "you can do it" mantra built from single Bible verses taken out of context. You won't find ideas here that run dry after you've read the last page, ideas that prove difficult to live out in the real world. Amena's writing is very different from these types of books: rather than a short-term motivational boost, she focuses on God's long-term ways of changing our old, undesired rhythms into new, refreshing ones.

What I loved about *Breaking Old Rhythms* is that Amena challenges us to not settle for less than the beauty of what God creates us each to be. I think we sometimes just settle into a rhythm of life because we think it would take too much effort or simply prove impossible to change. You will be inspired to rethink your dreams and reconsider the possibilities surrounding you as you read Amena's personal life experiences and are reminded of the power of God.

There is a fun Johnny Cash song that I like called "Get Rhythm." As the words of that song say, "Hey, get rhythm when you get the blues!" I am very thankful that Amena has challenged us to get not just any old rhythm, but to sync ourselves to God's rhythm for our lives.

I have had joy typing these words, knowing that your life will change as a result of what you are about to begin reading. Have a great experience within the pages of this book!

DAN KIMBALL

A WORD TO THE READER

I've read quite a few books on faith. Some were cliché-ridden, but a few really challenged me in my thoughts about God, church, faith, hope and love. My original idea for this book was a how-to guide on what to do when you find yourself in a rut. I started with an outline of thirteen chapters before realizing that eleven of them wouldn't work. God has a sense of humor in that the rhythm I thought would work for this book didn't keep time with what it really means to break old rhythms.

I've discovered there is no formula or equation for breaking rhythm. It is found in the way my grandmother can cook a whole meal with no recipe; in the way Grandmaster Flash took two records, a crossfader and his fingertips and made new music; the way Jesus without curriculum, bullet points or ProPresenter demonstrated to his disciples the way to really live.

As human beings we're all always searching. We want to be satisfied and accepted and fulfilled and loved. No person and no experience can do all of that for us except for God. But it takes most of us coming up empty several times before we realize it.

This book is about recognizing monotony when it's slowly stifling your ability to see anything but the trouble in front of you. About not letting the change of song keep you from dancing. About finding your rhythm even when you can't quite locate its rhyme or reason. About the journey of the search, and the answers and questions we find there. Here, we're not going to talk formula or bullet points; we'll talk mess and epiphany and how somewhere in the midst of it all we realize we're not alone. This God who many of us have tried to push off as some distant watchmaker, who creates creations and leaves them alone and wondering, is really a God who is present with us, who wants to know us, who wants us to know him.

A PRELUDE

We all have a rhythm we keep. I'm not talking about clapping on one/three or two/four. I'm not talking about bars of music or six/ eight time. I'm talking about a way of thinking, a routine, a comfort zone where we feel safe and secure, even when our safety and se- curity is built on a façade. Some of our rhythm we inherit from our family, some of it we choose and some of it we learn from our expe- riences. Sometimes life comes along with its requisite gut punches that knock the wind and the rhythm out of us. Or so it seems.

Now take a moment and wherever you are, clap your hands or snap your fingers ten times. Go on . . .

Did you notice you were starting to bob your head? That's what I hope these words will help you to do: Find a rhythm and, when necessary, break it.

ONE

FINDING YOUR RHYTHM

I was born of tambourine and handclap
Foot stomp on old wooden church floors
Learned to love a sound that came straight from James Brown
Not the Godfather of Soul
I'm talking about my father, whose soul is earth, wind & fire
Whose eyes are "shining stars for me to see"
Earphones bigger than six-month-old me
Placed around these little ears
So I could hear a slice of "what my life could truly be"

AMENA BROWN, *THE KEY OF G*

*T*he too-big headphones belonged to my dad, James Brown.
Yes, my dad's name is really James Brown. For years I have been
trying to convince people that this makes me the granddaughter
of soul—but no takers. When I was growing up, my dad listened
to funk and jazz, and he's been playing piano as long as I can
remember. Every time I hear Earth, Wind, & Fire's "Let's
Groove," I am transported back to the small living room in our
North Carolina townhome, my dad clad in doo-rag and short-
sleeved white T-shirt, my first time hearing the recording of a

horn section, layered vocals and a thumping bass line.

My mom played in the band during high school and was a lover of all things music: Prince, Michael Jackson, Tremaine Hawkins, Bob Marley, and Frankie Beverly and Maze. Eventually I got my own boom box and started to play the hip hop, jazz and soul tunes that moved me. Since before I said my first word, I've been following a rhythm. We all have.

THE POWER OF RHYTHM

I went to my first concert in Atlanta's Centennial Park in 2004. Admission was five dollars. Some friends and I met up, threw our blankets on the grass and waited for this new rapper named Kanye West to take the stage. He performed hits from his debut album *College Dropout*. My friends and I were all recent college grads so we could identify with Kanye's middle-class angst. Most of us were working far from dream jobs, doing what we could to make it between paychecks.

When Kanye performed his controversial hit "Jesus Walks," the audience went from bohemian blanket sitting to standing with hands in the air. I looked around at the crowd as the soldieresque background vocals and marching band percussion opened the song. Age, race, faith, skin color, fashion, economic status, didn't matter. The whole crowd was bobbing their heads, rocking their necks and bouncing their arms to the same beat. This was one of the first times I understood the power of rhythm.

We all have a rhythm we're used to—a tempo that goes beyond the kind of music we listen to. God gave each of us an internal rhythm. Put your hand over your heart, a hand over your wrist or two fingers on the side of your neck, and you'll discover you have your own internal click—a personal metronome that God thoughtfully put inside each of us. We find our rhythm in the way we like life to go, in the way we choose to love and allow ourselves to be loved, whether we like life to be easy, planned to the minute, exciting, adventurous or safe. Our rhythm is our life's cadence. It's something we follow, most times without even knowing it.

Take my single dating life, for example. I had a "rhythm" for dating guys who were really fun and creative and comedic—and emotionally unavailable and noncommittal. In a room full of fifty guys, I had great radar for picking that same man over and over again. Something about being with a guy who didn't really want to be with me was inherent in my rhythm.

When I write poems I typically write my first draft in pen while listening to John Coltrane. I've tried switching this up, writing to hip hop beats or soul music or guitar instrumentals, but my poems will not come out and dance unless Coltrane or Miles Davis is the Pied Piper. That's part of my rhythm.

During first grade, I lived with my grandma while my mom went through basic training in the army. My grandma played piano for the church choir, and she played those keys lively as if each one were its own bongo drum.

At my grandma's church, the youth choir wore black and white, the adult choir wore robes, all of the women in church wore long dresses and skirts with pantyhose and slips underneath, hair or wig pressed and curled, shoes and pocketbook to match, barely any make-up. The women taught me a rhythm. They showed me the powerful sound of voices lifted to God and feet patting out the beat in unison on the church's hardwood floors, but they also taught me a different rhythm: what it meant to be a church woman, a good girl. They taught me that good girls don't wear harlot-red lipstick or see-through blouses. They always wear slips, only speak when spoken to and keep their legs closed as if they were trying to keep a nickel tightly between their knees. They were teaching me the beginning of the rhythm of what I expected womanhood and Christianity to be.

JESUS IN THE ROOM WITH ME

With churchgoing parents and grandparents, I felt like I grew up around God. He went to my grandma's church, my aunt had his picture on her wall, and my mom listened to his music. God and I were more like acquaintances, friends of friends. We were never formally introduced, although I always had this feeling that maybe he wanted to have more than a passing conversation with me.

I always thought God was old, beige, bald, with a really long goatee, robed in white and barefoot. I always imagined Jesus as lots of paintings depict him: brown hair parted down the middle, wavy as if it had been loosely roller set, dressed in a white toga made of bed sheets and Birkenstocks because they seem like Jesus sandals. This God, this Jesus, always seemed stuffy, silent, distant, disconnected and disengaged. He never seemed like someone I could get close to.

My friend Kimberly asked me once if I could physically see Jesus in the room with me, what would I do. I tried to imagine him, but all my ideas came out cartoony. I told her I'd say hi to him, I'd even talk with him, but I wasn't sitting next to him. He could hold down his corner of the room and I'd hold down mine.

She told me she would sit in his lap, wrap her arms around him and lay her head on his chest. I couldn't imagine being that close to Jesus or that he would want to be that close to me. Since then, I have gone back to this question many times. Each time the scenario is different. Sometimes I am close enough to Jesus to lay my head on his shoulder, to listen to his heartbeat. Other times I am standing in the doorway of the room, unsure if I deserve to come in. Every time, I imagine Jesus with this look in his eyes as if he wants to be closer to me than I'll allow.

SINGING AND BELIEVING

A few years ago I was invited to share poetry at a restoration house for women recovering from drug addiction, alcoholism and prostitution. I wasn't sure what I'd have to say that would mean anything to the women there, but I went anyway. When I got there, the lady who facilitated the weekly Bible study opened the time as she usually did, playing a contemporary Christian song that you'd hear on the radio. They had no guitar player, no worship leader, just a song that I normally would have deemed cliché playing from an old boom box. There were eight or ten women in the room, and as the song played they started to sing. My stomach tightened in a way that caused my throat to close, and I knew I was going to cry. Not a pleasant, tears-rolling-gently-down-the-cheeks cry—I mean an ugly, can-hardly-talk-and-cry-at-the-same-time cry.

I realized these women really believed what they were singing about. I asked myself, *When was the last time I sang a song like this and believed the words I was singing?* To them, phrases including the words *set free, rescued, saved* weren't concepts to cognitively assent to or buzz words to throw around. God had really set them free from addiction, rescued them from street corners, saved them from a man's fist. I had a feeling God enjoyed listening to them sing, that their voices and hearts and notes mattered to him.

When they were done singing, I shared some poems and told some stories, but more than anything I thought about what my time with them had spoken to me. It made me question how long I had been running on empty. How long had God been commonplace to me? When did he stop being amazing, and what did it say about my heart that the Creator of the universe and Savior of the world was no longer awe-inspiring?

GOD'S RHYTHM

God has a rhythm, just as we do. God's rhythm is unchanging and eternal, full of love, hope and grace. Absolutely truthful, always available, incredibly powerful. If God had a rhythm, how could I find it? How was I missing it?

"My thoughts are not your thoughts," God says. "Neither are your ways my ways. . . . As the heavens are higher than the earth, so are my ways higher than your ways and my thoughts than your thoughts" (Isaiah 55:8-9). If God's thoughts and ways are higher than ours, then God's rhythm is probably vastly different from the rhythm I'm always trying so desperately to hold onto.

When I was growing up, a guest director came every year to direct our church choir for a special event. Before he would teach us new songs he would have all of us sing a particular note. He would walk through each row with his ear in front of us. If he passed by anyone who wasn't on the note, he would sing the note with him or her until that singer joined him in the correct pitch. I imagine God is a lot like that. His intention is not to break us for the sake of seeing us in pain or to correct us for the sake of ruining our fun. He's got a much bigger note he's trying to get us to hear, a strong rhythm he wants us to fall in line with. God's rhythm is not our rhythm. Neither is God's rhythm a flat line.

We are like instruments in God's orchestra. That means if we want to be a part of the symphony, we have to learn to follow God's beat.

We are like bones in a body—growing, stretching, discovering and sometimes breaking. God's rhythm is surgical, breaking, healing and mending where we have grown crooked.

We are like trees, extending our branches toward the light. God's rhythm is the post he ties us to, to make sure we grow straight, with roots growing deep into the soil.

Sometimes the rhythm I've built for myself falls short, peters out and gets fuzzy in the middle. Sometimes my rhythm shatters and breaks. It is these moments when I find God, when my ears are more attuned to his voice and character, when I can somehow hear his rhythm more clearly.

BREAKING RHYTHM

Read Isaiah 55:8-9. Reflect on some of the major decisions of your life: how have your ways been different from God's ways?

Which image of God is more appealing to you—God as orchestra conductor, surgeon or gardener? Why?

Think of a time when you felt the pain of a broken rhythm. How do you see God's involvement in that experience?

TWO

THE BLESSING OF IRRITATION

*Sometimes what seems like surrender isn't surrender at all.
It's about what's going on in our hearts. About seeing
clearly the way life is and accepting it and being
true to it, whatever the pain, because the pain
of not being true to it is far, far greater.*

TOM BOOKER, *THE HORSE WHISPERER*

*I*t starts with a little irritation. The beginning of being annoyed, unnerved, dissatisfied. This feeling grows to become frustration and starts boiling in your chest. This is when you realize you don't like where you are. You want to be somewhere else—anywhere else but here.

Sometimes I hate *here*. I think it should be thrown in as a bad word with all the other four-letter ones. *Here* is a second-place trophy, "Why can't you be more like your brother?" and "It'll happen when you least expect it" all rolled into one. When you're in high school you can't wait to get out of your parents' house. When you get to college, you can't wait to get into the real world. When you get into the real world, you can't wait to find your dream job. When you're single, you can't wait to get married.

When you get married, you can't wait to have kids. When you have kids, you can't wait for them to grow up and leave the house.

We feel restless and would rather avoid *here* by getting *there* as fast as we can. *Here* sucks. It's not back then, not quite there yet. *Here* can be purgatory, your own version of Dante's *Inferno*. *Here* is like sitting at a bus stop with your bags packed but no idea when your bus will arrive or where it might take you.

Here can seem so slow-moving. It's not as glorified as the past but not as mysterious as the future. The past is the slick-talking bad boy who has wit to match all of your fears and inhibitions. The future is a suit-wearing professional, promising you the world without saying much about how you'll get there. The present wears nerdy, nearsighted glasses and has a pocket protector full of tools for managing your time and creative process.

The tricky thing about *here* is that it only lasts for a moment. In a little while, our current life and circumstances will be the past. If we spend our present wishing we were in the past or hoping so hard for our future, we miss appreciating what we have and gaining the most from where we are.

Here is where we discover our rhythm.

THE PRINCESS AND THE PEA

When I was just a couple of years out of college, I fell in love with New York City. I had an opportunity to move there and serve in a missions project. I also had an opportunity to take a job in Atlanta in corporate America working as a writer. Should I throw caution to the wind, embrace being broke and move to New York where I'd have to live with seventeen roommates in a three-square-foot apartment and work six jobs to make a living? Should I resign myself to a life of humdrum and boredom by taking a stuffy corporate job? Was the broke-ness worth the proximity to Broadway and the chance to be discovered? Was the practicality of the job worth financial stability?

I was twenty-five years old with more than $30,000 in student loan debt that could be deferred no longer. I chose the corporate job, broke up with New York, asked if we could just be friends, promising we'd get back together someday. I took what felt like my first real job, as a business writer for a Fortune 500 company. I had even been given the title of Communications Specialist, which sounded much better than my previous job titles: smoothie maker, phone answerer and calendar seller.

For the first few months, I loved the job. I loved the size and regularity of the paycheck. I loved that I was actually getting paid to do what I'd studied in college. I loved that I sounded like a professional when I told other people what I did for a living. But after some months on the job, I realized I hadn't technically been hired to write; I had been hired to do a lot of rewriting and revising of things that had already been written. My boss didn't really want me to be creative; he wanted me to write plainly, in the same voice that the materials had been written in twenty years before.

I felt like a traitor, a sellout of the creative race, choosing to pay my bills by working for the man. My view of my cubicle went from "bright and full of future" to "graveyard of dead dreams" every time I walked into our department.

A few weeks later, to keep myself from cursing on my way home from work during rush hour, I called my mom.

"How's your job going?" she asked.

"It's okay so far. I just hope I made the right decision. I don't want to get caught up in the steady paycheck of this job and forget that I'm a creative person."

"Do you remember the story of the Princess and the Pea?"

"Yeah," I said, thinking this wasn't the best time for her to recount Hans Christian Andersen fairy tales.

"Well, I think this job will be just enough irritation to keep you passionate about what you really love."

Once upon a time there was a prince looking for a princess. He searched high and low and couldn't find one to his liking. Suddenly, on a dark and stormy night, a drenched and forlorn girl showed up at the castle door. (Okay, maybe Hans wasn't best known for his intricately constructed plots, nevertheless go with me here.) She called herself a princess, but the prince's mother, the queen, didn't quite believe her.

The queen thought of the perfect way to find out the truth. She placed a pea on the girl's bed, then piled twenty mattresses and twenty down bedspreads on top of it. If the girl slept through the night, the queen reasoned, she was really no princess at all; her pampered upbringing would cause her to notice even the slightest interruption in her bed linens.

The princess awoke the next morning and reported having a dreadful sleep. The prince had found his princess after all.

As it turned out, my mom was right: I was the princess, and the job I came to hate was the pea. I suppose I was hoping that my dream job, my prince, would find me.

Whoever you are, dear reader, today—at least while you're reading this chapter—you're the princess. Your "pea"—your source of irritation—could be a job, a relationship, a success, a failure or an incessant gnawing that you want to be more, be better.

Irritation is the beginning of breaking rhythm. It's that small crack in the foundation of your comfort zone. It's when you wake up with cold feet and realize you've outgrown your safety blanket. It's when you finally realize you can't stomach *here* anymore.

THE IRRITANT

I could hardly stomach Mondays anymore. Then my inability to stomach the first day of the workweek started bleeding over into Sunday night. My tummy turned slow flips, which became knots as I thought about donning my corporate attire and pretending for most of the day that I was happy.

My cubicle became a nuisance. Its blank, thin walls mocked me. I'd refused to decorate or hang pictures of my family there. I didn't want this place to feel anything like home. Neutral things started to annoy me—all of the ad nauseum acronyms that came with my job, the quarterly reviews, department meetings, even the structure of how memos were written unraveled my anger.

For me, my irritant was a job, but irritants come in all shapes, sorts and sizes. Sometimes we find irritants in our relationships, in our voyeuristic observations of the successes or failures of others, in seeing a lie and desperately wanting the truth to be told, in our perception of how we are being viewed or treated, in the injustice we witness with no one to champion its solution. Irritants are mere symptoms. They force us to address them.

The most lasting way to rid ourselves of an irritant is not to simply quit our jobs, cut people off or remove ourselves from situations. Instead we must first dig—we must find the root of what our irritant is telling us we want. Sometimes what we want could be good: fulfillment, love or justice. Sometimes what we want is not good: to be better than someone else or to have what someone else has.

More than irritation shows us about other people or our circumstances, it shows us a true picture of ourselves and our own motives. Our irritation is rarely about our job, our relationship or any external happening. Irritation shines a bright light on something that lives in us all along. It is the ultimate truth serum, showing us the true underlying meter of our hearts and whether our pulse is truly aligned with God's.

GOD'S PURPOSE FOR IRRITATION

I've learned that sometimes God is in the irritation. Sometimes God likes to shake things up. (Gasp!) Sometimes God likes to make us uncomfortable—not because he's sadistic and gets a thrill

out of our tears and frustration but because he knows most of the
• time irritation is the best way to get our attention. Frustration and
irritation are great motivators. It turns out they both have big feet
that gravitate toward kicking us in the rear end. God knows that
irritation, frustration, even pain and discomfort make our lives
and our prayers more honest.

Hannah badly wanted to have a baby. She prayed so crazily that
her priest accused her of being drunk. Meanwhile, Hannah had to
watch her husband's other wife birth him children as easily as she
got up in the morning (1 Samuel 1:1-14).

Joseph had a fantastic dream that he was going to become
somebody great and rule over his brothers. They threw him into a
well and sold him into slavery. He went on to serve a sentence for a
crime he didn't commit. Someone promised to plead his case and
then waited two years to deliver on that promise (Genesis 37–40).

Abraham and Sarah waited for decades to have children; they
were old enough to be somebody's great-great-great-grandparents
before God promised that they would birth a "nation." And then,
once they had a child together, God told Abraham to take this
long-awaited son and sacrifice him on an altar (Genesis 15–22).

Irritated yet? From miserable first dates, dead-end jobs, jealousy
at the success of others, discouragement from criticism or the
short-lived high of pride from accolades, irritation doesn't just
want to be our teacher, irritation wants to be our boot-camp drill
sergeant. And we will say, "Yes sergeant," or we will get down and
give irritation some push-ups.

God likes irritation—not because it hurts us but because it
always brings us to the place he wants us to be: at the end of ourselves, at the beginning of him. The question is, When God allows
us to be irritated, what is he trying to tell us? What is he trying to
say? What does he want from us?

Maybe God wants to teach us discipline, compassion, love,

grace, perseverance, surrender. Maybe he wants us to get up and do something instead of thinking or talking about it. Maybe he wants us to stop hiding our talents and who we are and be who he created us to be. Maybe he wants us to stop being afraid of what people might think, to stop giving other people's voices more weight than we give his. Maybe he wants us to be still and listen. Whatever it is he wants to say, you will keep being irritated until he gets his point across. Which means for us hardheaded people, we could be irritated a long time.

THE COST OF IRRITATION

When I buy things, I hold onto them, use them and run them into the ground. I bought a pair of sneakers once and figured out how to match them to almost every outfit in my closet, no matter how formal or casual, until my friend Kimberly finally had a fashion intervention with me. She discussed the virtue of seasonal shoes and purchasing footwear based on color and occasion.

I drag, throw around and carry purses and laptop bags until the shoulder straps disintegrate and the handles shred. I carried around an Apple iBook G4 computer and a flip cell phone until the people who loved me finally sat me down and explained that these days they have computers that don't weigh as much as a kindergartener and that there are phones with screens and keypads so when I'm typing a text message I don't have to press a number three times for each letter.

My car has been known to squeak, squeal and screech to the dismay and distraction of my fellow drivers and neighbors. Eventually I would get worried enough to get it checked out. Sometimes the tires were bald, the oil was long overdue for changing, or the brake rotors were creating their own cloud of powder from their friction with each other. Mechanics would shake their heads as they showed me my dirty air filters.

This changed when my husband, Matt, and I started dating. He had walked me up to my doorstep and was telling me about his plans for the next day (something we typically did to extend our date as long as possible). I had plans to write and have coffee with a friend; he was going to get his oil changed and head to work.

"Oh yeah. I need to get my oil changed too," I said.

To me, this comment was in the same category as, "Oh yeah, I need to organize my closet too." It sounded nifty to say, but I had no plans to act on it any time soon in real life.

"When was the last time you got your oil changed?" he asked.

I responded with a combination of incoherent consonants.

He looked at me with the sweetest eyes but said with the firmest voice, "Your oil needs to be changed. I'm gonna take care of it."

"No, no, I'll do it," said the girl who'd never had a boyfriend offer to take care of her car.

I thought we had agreed that sometime in the near (possibly, maybe) future I would take my car to Jiffy Lube. The next morning, however, I realized we had not agreed to any such thing. It was 8 a.m. and he was calling my phone.

"Hello?" I said, trying to disguise my completely asleep voice.

"Good morning. I'm on the way to pick up your car."

This man was serious. And now I had to figure out a way to look cute *and* like I just woke up. I met him at the door and handed him my keys; within the hour, he returned my car, oil changed. He gave me my keys and a lecture before he headed off to work.

"It's important to get your oil changed regularly. If you wait to take care of it until it starts making noise, it's going to cost you more and more," he said.

I nodded.

"But I'm gonna take care of that now. Have a great day!" he said.

And with that he kissed my cheek and headed off to work, gaining my respect and my heart.

Irritation is like the screeching noise your car makes that sends you to the mechanic, like the sharp, consistent pain that makes you go to the doctor. It is the thing that will keep bothering you until you do something about it. Matt was right: the longer we wait to listen to those out-of-tune sounds our lives make, the more it will cost us. Don't wait until the sound of irritation in your life is banging so loudly, your eardrums are stinging. Irritation is God's alarm clock. It's how he calls us to wake up, to respond, to change.

Breaking Rhythm

What is irritating you lately? Why?

How might this irritation be a blessing?

What action might your irritation be calling you to?

THREE

THE RHYTHM OF FIGHTING

Something is different. Anything different is good.

PHIL, GROUNDHOG DAY

*B*y the time I got settled into my corporate job, my rhythm had about as much variation as the movie *Groundhog Day*. In that film, every morning at 6 a.m., a weatherman named Phil (played by Bill Murray) wakes up to Sonny and Cher singing "I Got You Babe." Every day is Groundhog Day. Phil is forced to relive the same day over and over again until he decides to approach life differently.

I was living my life on autopilot, not expecting much and not gaining much. I had accepted this and assumed it was growing up: this was adulthood. I was wearing the same combination of black pants, skirts, ugly shoes and boxy blazers. Driving the same congested highway to work, arriving with the same terrible attitude, dropping my stuff in the same cubicle and taking the same way-too-long breakfast break. Same snare kick. Same annoying regularity of the dance between my alarm clock and my snooze button.

Ever since I've had a job, I've taken my birthday as a holiday—a personal day, PTO. While working in corporate America, I decided to use that day off each year to meet with someone who could encourage me in the pursuit of my dreams. One year, a few weeks before my birthday, I was asked to be a part of a gala to raise money for a nonprofit organization in Atlanta. Russ and Jonathan were spearheading the event and others like it. I wanted to hear more about their passion for fighting injustice through cool events, and they wanted to hear more about poetry and performance art, so I invited them to my annual birthday coffee. The three of us cupped our hands around mugs of hot and strong espresso at Octane Coffee and told our stories.

I told them about spoken word, hip hop and poetry. They told me about nonprofits, about trying to engage a generation into being givers. Russ told a story they'd heard recently about Bruce Lee's obsession with drumming and rhythm.

A martial arts pioneer, Lee reasoned that if he could learn to fight with the same irregular rhythm some drummers used, his opponents would never guess which way he was coming from. Russ went on to elaborate on how we all get stuck in our everyday, mundane, humdrum routines. He turned to me and said, "So, what do you think would be your first step in switching rhythms?"

Up to this point the conversation had been cool, deep, intellectual—artistic even. But now I said aloud what I'd never said before: "To leave my job."

I was scared to death of that statement, even more scared that I had just articulated something I'd been feeling for the past several months and attempting to bury. Russ was stepping over the line. He was turning the conversation from idealistic to realistic, forcing me to put the metaphor of his story into action.

Broken Rhythm

If the rhythm has been well established, there is a tendency to continue the sequence of the movement.

Bruce Lee, *Bruce Lee's Fighting Method*

———— ∞∞ ————

Most of us like our rhythm familiar. We like for the beat to be something we recognize. We typically aren't excited to go to a concert because we can't wait to hear music we've never heard before. We like music concerts because we want to hear a live version of the songs we already know. In music and in life, once we've established a rhythm, it can be hard to break it.

I decided to study up on Bruce Lee since the only reference I knew of him was from spoof movie *I'm Gonna Git You Sucka*, where Kung Fu Joe referred to Bruce Lee as his teacher and carried a framed picture of him around his neck the entire film.

Martial artist, philosopher and actor Bruce Lee created his own martial art, Jeet Kune Do, which includes the principle of Broken Rhythm. He describes it this way:

> Ordinarily, two fighters of equal ability can follow each other's movements and, unless there is a considerable difference in speed, they are very likely to stalemate each other. However, when the rhythm is broken, speed is no longer the primary element in the success of the attack or counterattack. . . . The man who can break this rhythm by a light hesitation or an unexpected movement can now score an attack or counterattack with only moderate speed; his opponent is motorset to continue with the previous rhythm, and before he can adjust himself to the change, he has been hit.

I've never been a good fighter. My arms have always been slight, skinny, with droopy Olive Oyl muscles. The only fight I ever won was against my brother, Robert. I was nine, and he was seven. I'd watched enough World Wrestling Federation on TV to know how to bear hug him as a wrestling move. I basically squeezed my arms around him until his face turned red. This tactic worked, along with taunting about how I was the big sister and I'd always be bigger—until a few summers went by and my little brother towered over me by a foot and a half. So at this point, winning fights with a sibling doesn't count. The closest I came to a real fight wasn't even a fight of my own.

LINEBACKER VS. LITTLE OPPONENT

When I was in the fifth grade, I was selected to be a patrol. My elementary school was about three blocks away from the apartment my mom and I lived in. If you were accepted into the patrol program you received a safety orange sash and belt that crossed your chest and waist like a seatbelt, plus a smart silver badge. This made you official.

My post was at the beginning of the path that led to school from behind the field and playground, closer to our apartment complex than the school. Our school bully, Tiffany, took advantage of this by staging fights at my post. Tiffany might as well have been a linebacker. She was five times my size, and I feared she could eat me and leave nothing but a yellow feather floating in the air as if I were Tweety and she were Sylvester.

The other trouble with Tiffany was that she came from a family of bullies. If she didn't sufficiently conquer her prey, her father (who could have been an Andre the Giant look-alike) and linebacker siblings would show up at my corner prepared for the beat down.

One dreary, chilly morning I saw Tiffany and her dad crossing the street toward my post. I thought to remind them to use the sidewalk instead of jaywalking a busy four-lane street, but the size of their shoulders made me take my chances with any vehicle that would dare tangle with them.

Tiffany's opponent was waiting near me, chest poked out but eyes slightly watering. I wanted to tell her, "Run! Don't do this! You don't have to prove anything to this linebacker!" But it was too late; word on her meeting Tiffany was already out. She had to follow through. I was torn between running back to the school to get help and not wanting to leave Little Opponent by herself. I also did not want to be left dangling on the cliffhanger of how Tiffany would beat this girl down. So I stayed, watching in slow motion with a chill in my back as a cold wind blew and Tiffany and her huge father arrived on the sidewalk.

Little Opponent completed about two sentences of talking trash before tears started flying into the cold wind. She realized what she was up against. I didn't understand why she hadn't shown up on the block with a family member. Even an older sister or brother could have gotten some punches in. Everybody knew that if Tiffany was meeting you at the school path it wasn't the first time she'd tussled with you. Hadn't Little Opponent learned?

The answer was clearly no as Tiffany's fist railed on Little Opponent. My heart was jumping quick double-dutch in my chest; I was afraid Tiffany's dad would get in the mix and attempt to beat somebody else's child. Then I realized his role here. He was a coach, and these schoolyard fights were scrimmages. Tiffany was Rocky Balboa and her dad was old Mickey Goldmill, shouting out tips from the grassy patch beside the sidewalk about how she could most effectively beat this girl up.

There was no bloodshed. Little Opponent eventually became no fun to Linebacker Tiffany and family because she cowered on the sidewalk in the fetal position to prevent too many body hits. Old Mickey felt satisfied with Tiffany's hits that day, and they tramped back across the street as if school wasn't starting in twenty minutes.

Little Opponent made her way to school, and a few minutes later I did too. I can't remember her face or name, can't remember if I told my teachers when we got to school. I decided then that I wanted nothing of a fistfight.

ME VS. ME

In literature, there are five basic types of conflict: man versus man, man versus society, man versus nature, man versus fate, and man versus himself. Most of my conflicts fall under that last category. Woman versus herself.

Fighting seems to be a way of life. We fight to be normal and then fight to be unique and original. We fight to be loved and then sometimes fight off the best of love when it comes to us. We fight for the respect of others when we don't respect them or ourselves.

The apostle Paul believed there's such a thing as a "good fight": "Pursue righteousness, godliness, faith, love, endurance and gentleness. Fight the good fight of the faith. Take hold of the eternal life to which you were called" (1 Timothy 6:11-12). To fight for something means we deem it worth risking our safety for, means we care more about defeating our opponent than about how we look or what we could stand to lose. It means there is such a thing as a "bad fight"—things we fight for that aren't worth it, like earning people's approval, impressing people, coming off as better than anyone else. Those fights are never worth it. Fighting to be your best, to be yourself, not to settle, to do what's right, to live the life God calls us to—that is a worthy fight.

Some days my critical inner voice comes storming into my mind, looking for a fight. She's accompanied by her big daddy, Insecurity. Some days all I can do is curl up, cover my liver and kidneys, and hope for the best.

But it would stand to reason that if there is a rhythm to how a fighter shuffles his feet, swings his jabs or punches his hits, then maybe there is a rhythm to how we live, believe, hope and surrender—and also a rhythm to how and when we don't. Maybe by switching up our thought patterns we can catch our inner voice off guard and gain the advantage over it. Learning from Bruce Lee hasn't given me the desire to pummel anyone. If anything, it has made me want to fight the things inside me: selfishness, pride, small thinking, my seeming inability to trust God with the things that worry me.

Navigating a New Normal

The words I said aloud to Russ and Jonathan haunted me each day as I returned to my cubicle. I was single, didn't have any children and realized if I didn't leave this dream cemetery of a job I never would because the more responsibilities I had the less likely I'd be to take the risk of pursuing my dreams.

So at the end of a two-year stint, a few months after I'd first uttered the words "leave my job" and right after my Christmas bonus hit my bank account, I put in my two-week notice. By then I had been traveling off and on performing poetry, and had to turn down some dates because I couldn't get the time off work. I thought this meant that as soon as I quit my cushy corporate gig, the floodgates would open up and I'd have so many booking requests I wouldn't know how to handle them all.

When you break an old rhythm, you have to learn a new normal. For years I had been used to having a boss or a supervisor tell me what to do, when and how to do it. I was used to working for companies that were already established. Now I was the only one to tell me what to do.

I went from working on a team to a one-woman operation, from a steady paycheck to a highly irregular one. No more boxy blazers, no cubicle, just my sweats and my dining room table posing as a desk. When I was still resting in the safety of my corporate job, I imagined I was making a mere career transition; in actuality I was starting over, building something from the ground up.

I quickly discovered I wasn't ready. Fighters prepare, train, discipline their exercise and eating habits, focus their mind on the win. Marathon runners don't decide a couple of days before the race to start jogging. It takes weeks of preparation to ready the body and the mind for the trail ahead. Jesus advised his disciples to anticipate the cost of following him. "Suppose one of you wants to build a tower. Won't you first sit down and estimate the cost to see if you have enough money to complete it? For if you lay the foundation and are not able to finish it, everyone who sees it will ridicule you, saying, 'This person began to build and wasn't able to finish'" (Luke 14:28-30).

I was treating my new full-time artist job as a vacation instead of a vocation. I went to the movies or grabbed dinner with the guy I was dating any time the mood suited me, assuming that work would find me.

It took breaking up, going broke and moving out for me to learn a valuable lesson about breaking an old rhythm: *prepare yourself.* Listen closely for the new rhythm by which you'll be living. Learn its nuance; prepare your mind, heart and soul for the journey ahead.

WHEN THE RHYTHM BREAKS YOU

The first year of my new normal was more difficult than anticipated. My bonus and all other cash had run out, my credit card was maxed out, I was afraid to answer my phone for all the bill collectors calling and wanting their share of the zero I had in my bank account, and there were few gigs in sight. I suffered what felt like a seismic relationship breakup, and then, just as I began to feel like I had solid footing, I reconnected with "the one who got away."

Most of us have that one person in our past that we messed up our chances with. I'll call him Steinbeck, as he is the only reason I finished the book *East of Eden.*

Steinbeck had given me a chance in the past, when I was in my mid-twenties, young and naïve and selfish. Steinbeck had been ready to get married. He was in his early thirties, settled in his career, growing in his relationship with Jesus. All he was missing was the Mrs. I had just discovered I was cute and wanted to share that fact with as many takers as I could find. To me, it wasn't time to settle down—it was time to nab as many dates with various suitors as possible. Over a candlelit dinner at a jazz spot, I told Steinbeck so. Told him I thought he was awesome, that I loved his heart, that any woman who got him would have a great man on her hands, but I just wanted to be friends. Nicer to me than he probably should have been, he paid the expensive check, thanked me for my honesty, walked me to my car and hugged me good night without cursing me or the day I was born.

Shortly after this, Steinbeck moved away to pursue his dreams and higher education. We lost touch because in my absence he probably did curse me and the day I was born, and because I respected his ability to do so.

As the years went by, I realized how hurtful I'd been. I also realized, after dating several men of the trifling sort, how I had taken Steinbeck and his gentlemanly ways for granted. So when he called on New Year's Eve and said he was coming back to town, had a performance and wanted me to come check it out, I was more than thrilled and ready to make up for my wanton ways. We spent the New Year greeting old friends and stayed up for hours talking at my apartment while I cooked collard greens for New Year's dinner with my family.

We talked about the future: Steinbeck was moving to New York to continue his career. I had been thinking about moving there too and hoped that if we had a future maybe I'd have even more reason to pack up my things and start a new life. We left the night open-ended—no promises, no strings attached. But I had a dangerous new companion: hope. Maybe this was my chance to make this right. Maybe this was the man I was supposed to marry.

As things were going downhill for me financially, the one thing I was holding onto was the hope that Steinbeck and I would instantly become characters in a Renee Zellweger chick flick. I'd become a NY girl, move into a penthouse apartment, furnished, including Carrie's shoe collection from *Sex and the City*. We'd get married and have New York babies, whatever that means.

Months passed with no word from Steinbeck. I did all that a girl who was trying to be a lady could do, sent a sweet text or two, left a cool voicemail that sort of said, "Hey, I want you to call me, but you know when you have time, because you know, I know you're busy and totally respect that even though it would be, you know, the light of my life if you would call me whenever you get a spare minute, but, you know, no pressure or anything."

While waiting for a return call from Steinbeck, I kept myself busy avoiding the bill collector's calls about my car. I didn't have the money to make my car payment, hadn't had the money for over sixty days. The nice customer service rep was no longer leaving voicemail messages. I had been handed over to the "We will tell you how much we hate you to make you pay" customer service reps. They gave me an ultimatum: Pay up or we repo.

One sad day, when I was lying on my uncomfortable couch contemplating the shambles of my life, my phone rang. All of the sunshine seemed to light up my living room when I saw it was Steinbeck's name on my phone.

I was so excited, thinking, *Thank you for rescuing me from the doldrums of my life with a little romance.* He had finished a show recently, and I was excited to hear his voice, to have some hope in a very doubtful couple of weeks.

Scene.

Cell phone rings. Amena's heart jumps at seeing Steinbeck's name on her phone.

Amena: Heeeeey!

Steinbeck: Hey, how are you?

Amena: I'm good. How are you?! Tell me everything! How did the show go?

Steinbeck: The show was amazing! Had some issues with the director because she didn't know what she was doing, but the show turned out so well. My co-star and I have been dating for a month, and that's been going even better than the show.

Amena's heart goes to beating like it's going to jump out of her chest and become a big mess on the floor of her living room. Amena tries to pull herself together.

Amena: Wow, well, good stuff.

Amena says this because she feels it will go over better than "Expletive, expletive, expletive."

Scene.

I had planned to swap cars with my best friend and her husband that night, an attempt to dodge the repo. Of course, it was raining as I drove to their place. It was also raining tears all over my face. I experienced a strange combination of peace and sadness. I knew that I would be the ultimate hypocrite to balk at the abrupt way he announced his new relationship, since I chose to end our time dating at what was supposed to be a candlelit, romantic dinner. These facts did not alleviate the hurt I was feeling, but they helped me to accept the scene I had been given. Steinbeck, after all, deserved to be happy, deserved to be with someone who didn't take years to figure out he was worth it.

I wondered, *How did my life go so quickly from hopeful and exciting with dreams, to dashed dating life, being broke and forced to ask for the kind of help that makes me feel like less than a person?* I got to my friends' house, and they did what loving friends do. Told me they loved me, that I would make it, that I would survive this, that times like this happen to everyone, that they didn't think any less of me and I didn't need to think any less of myself.

For me, the beat down happened financially and romantically simultaneously—and if I could have found one more word to rhyme with that I would have, but I digress. I went broke and suffered heartbreak within months. My car had nearly been taken away from me forever. All I knew to do was lie down on my couch and cry. This would have been a great time to freak out and cuss God out. I was honestly starting to wonder if God even liked me. I mean, I knew from Scripture that he loved me because he is love and there is no way for him to be anything else. But he never promised he had to like us. I just couldn't see how he could leave my dating life in shambles, watch me go broke trying to pursue the dream I thought he'd given to me and still like me. It's hard to understand God, mostly because our brains are just too small, but also because we can't see as much as he sees. Can't see his plans and how his storylines come together in the end.

The other difficult thing about the beat down is that it's lonely. No amount of rubs on the back or well-intentioned words can make you feel as if anyone really understands anything you're going through. The loss of my grandparents within months of each other; moving, unpacking and losing old friends to make new ones; a career of traveling the same planes that used to shuttle me between the houses of my two parents; falling in love only to be dealt my deepest broken heart; pursuing my dream only to fail miserably at it—I'm sure we all have stories like these. These are the places where life dealt us a swift but powerful blow to the gut, knocking the breath out of our very lungs and then forcing us to stand up, take it and continue to live. These moments are inevitable. The difficult part about when our rhythm is broken is that the breaking is out of our control. What do you do when things you can't control change around you, leaving you broken, wounded and shaken?

THE AFTERMATH OF THE BEAT DOWN

Typically my first question is why. Why me? And then, why, God? Why do YOU do this to me? Yes, I whine, complain and throw temper tantrums. God can seem so silent when the rhythm is breaking. He seems suddenly mute in a time when I really need to hear him speak and explain to me why all of this is happening. I want him to tell me what I'm supposed to gain from this and how I'm supposed to go on and live, to try and not give up. When the rhythm breaks you, it makes you want to quit and question everything you ever staked your life on.

Anytime in life when I have experienced the beat down, my relationship with God gets very honest. When I've been hurt, disappointed, blindsided, I cut through all the formalities and falsehoods pretty quickly and get straight down to just asking God to HELP ME. And he always does. And sometimes that doesn't look like immediately paying the bills or quickly sending a date or making my hips looks like Beyoncé's, but he always helps. Whether it's helping me to remember that no matter how lonely I feel I'm not walking through anything by myself, that he's always with me; or whether it's him helping me to remember that it's okay when I'm weak because he is more than strong enough—not just strong enough for me, but strong enough to handle the weakness of the whole world.

The irony and beauty of following God is that in the middle of each panic is peace. The peace comes because, though you may not know what's going to happen or how the plotline of your life will unfold or if you'll ever find love again or if you'll ever be able to pay those bills piling up on the table, you do know one thing— one thing you can be sure of. God knows all and sees all, which means he knows you and sees you. Times like these force us not to focus on our circumstances but instead to look at the One who knows and has control over them.

If we let it, the beat down can make us stronger, can tell us what we really believe. Because it's easy to believe that God provides when you've got a steady paycheck, and it's easy to accept that love is patient and kind and available when you have someone else's hand to hold, when all the stoplights seem to be green, when everyday things seem to come together as planned and expected. But it's a whole lot more difficult to believe in God when things don't make sense, when loss and confusion crowd in. That's when we know if we really believe God like we say we do.

In some cases the change in our rhythm that comes with the beat down breaks us. We're left puzzled, stuck and sometimes without motivation to begin again. But you don't get to quit because it's tough, uncomfortable or inconvenient. There are some times in life when you need to fight to the finish. Each time you do prepares you for the next time you feel life is closing in on you and teaches you to trust the One who knows all things. The beat down is, sometimes, a means to breaking rhythm.

When the beat down happens in my life, I try to remember a few things. It's okay to hurt, to be disappointed and to wish things were different. That doesn't make you weak or mean that you don't have faith. It means you're human. I'm so thankful that God is well aware of that. It's part of why Jesus came, because he wanted to be able to look at us and say, "I know exactly how you feel." And he does—no matter how you feel, what you've done or what's been done to you.

It's also okay to ask for help.

Two are better than one,
because they have a good return for their labor:
If either of them falls down,
one can help the other up.
But pity anyone who falls
and has no one to help them up.
Though one may be overpowered,
two can defend themselves.
A cord of three strands is not quickly broken.
(Ecclesiastes 4:9-10, 12)

Sometimes we can get some weird personal glory from trying to be a martyr and go through things alone. No matter what happens in your life, you're never just a victim. Your life isn't built on the things that happen to you. It's also built on the person you chose to become because of or in spite of those things. We grow when other people help us, when we can be humble enough and real enough to say, "Life is hard, I'm overwhelmed, I don't know how much more I can take," and have someone else say, "I understand, I'm here."

Breaking rhythm is about change, about dealing with delay, pause, surprise and all of the moments when life doesn't unfold the way we want or expect. God always knows and always has a plan. A friend of mine used to pray, "Thank you, God, that nothing occurs to you."

The problem comes in when my plan is way different from his. I must think I'm pretty smart, to think I could have my whole life figured out, handle all my relationships and know exactly what to say and do at any given moment. God breaks my rhythm when he lets me see the distance between his plans for me and my plans for myself, the gap between his will and mine.

Training for a fight, recovering from a defeat, walking your way to a new normal—all have a beat. It may not be the rhythm you're used to. It may not even be a rhythm you like, but give it a listen. Tune your soul to its rise and fall. You may find that your heart has its own way of hearing the music the ultimate Composer is creating.

Breaking Rhythm

🌿 Watch a boxing or martial arts match. Keep an eye out for broken rhythms. How do they change the dynamic of the match?

🌿 Describe a time when you experienced the beat down. What did it teach you about yourself? About God?

🌿 How could you better navigate your new normal?

FOUR

IF GOD IS A DJ

DJing is not just about choosing a few tunes. It is about generating shared moods; it's about understanding the feelings of a group of people and directing them to a better place. In the hands of a master, records become the tools for rituals of a spiritual communion that for many people are the most powerful events in their lives.

BILL BREWSTER AND FRANK BROUGHTON,
LAST NIGHT A DJ SAVED MY LIFE

learned a lot about God from DJing, from standing in a smoky club with liquor and condensation gracing the floor and messing up many a nice pair of shoes. Some of my friends find that God speaks to them in the mountains, on the beach or in the country. God often speaks to me through songs and live musical experiences. Kelly Clarkson's "Breakaway" became my anthem for refusing to let fear keep me from the freedom God has given to me. India.Arie's "Strength, Courage, and Wisdom" has been God's reminder to me that having faith requires action; the song has helped to teach me the balance between trusting, surrendering and lettings things be. Watching the interplay between an upright bassist, a keys player and a trumpet player—the way they listen to each other, riff off one another's notes and complement each other's solos—echoes Jesus' humility to me, the mystery and holiness of the Trinity, and the way prayer is a dialogue between the infinite and the finite. I can see God more clearly when I imagine him a grand conductor, a composer, a painter and creator of masterpieces, a turntablist.

Before I left my corporate job, I decided that since my work was not creative, I needed another outlet. I experimented with becoming a music journalist. I had taken a journalism class in college—the kind where we wrote headlines and short articles in the computer lab and our professor perused the aisles and our writing skills. She came to my desk, peered over my shoulder and said, "You write ear copy instead of eye copy," and walked to the next student's desk.

To my insecure writer self, this was not a compliment. I basically thought she was saying I wasn't going to make a good journalist, that my poetry background had ruined my ability to write concisely or succinctly, as a journalist should. So I gave up on that and kept my eyes on becoming the next Toni Morrison.

I realized years later what she meant, that I wrote things not for how they read on paper but for how they sounded aloud. I took on the volunteer job of writing for a couple of local newsletters and magazines in Atlanta. My assignments typically involved covering music shows, critiquing or celebrating what I saw, giving the reader the experience of what it felt like to have attended the event in person, and if the artists were really good, spreading the word about them.

I wrote about emcees, singer/songwriters and musicians. This lead me to an event called the Main Ingredient, spearheaded by D.R.E.S. tha BEATnik, an emcee and event host who could beat box, promote and keep the party hype. This was the first time I experienced two things: seeing a set of turntables up close and seeing the DJ as a performing artist.

Of course, I'd seen a record player and learned how to use one at about eight years old when my mom bought me my first records: Kid 'n Play's *2 Hype*, Michael Jackson's *Bad* and The Boys' debut LP, *A Message from the Boys*. But I had never watched a DJ rock the party up close. The Main Ingredient was at the MJQ Concourse in Atlanta, an underground club in the literal and figurative sense. You paid at the door and walked down a dark ramp into the club toward a glowing blue bar in the center of the room. The rest was dance floor. Instead of having mics for performers or drum set and amps set up for a band, the center stage was filled with two sets of turntables. The night would feature three main DJs with some surprise guests in between: DJ Scooter, DJ Majestik and DJ Scizzahands.

That was the first time I ever watched a DJ work or realized the relationship between DJ and audience, the artistry of record scratching, song mixing and remixing. I watched the DJs rotate positions on the turntables, watched the audience respond with excitement, anticipation and surprise at not knowing what the DJ would do next. We'd hear a familiar song, and then the DJ would flip it with a fresh beat underneath, or focus on just a few lines of the song, or mix out the music and place an emcee's vocals, a cappella, on top of a totally different beat.

This is when I realized that DJs at their best were not just for background music or to play some greatest hits. DJs are artists, composers, remixers. In some ways their turntables are their instruments.

DJ is an acronym for disc jockey. A DJ's job is to take a cadre of songs, mix them together, matching beats and melodies so the audience has a seamless, nonstop dancing experience. The DJ found a new use for the "break, a jazz term for the dance record where the melody takes a rest and the drummer cuts loose," according to Bill Brewster and Frank Broughton, authors of *Last*

Night a DJ Saved My Life: The History of the Disc Jockey. DJs became masters of the breakbeat: a rhythm that is broken, syncopated or abstract, used in funk, jazz, hip hop and drum 'n' bass.

This established the term *breaking,* where dancers created gymnastic, staccato and smooth movements on the break. These dancers were known to wait on the wall in break-boy or break-girl (also known as b-boy/b-girl) stance until the break came in. The earliest hip hop DJs created full songs of the breaks to keep the people dancing instead of making the b-boys and b-girls wait. The job of the masterful DJ was to take a bunch of breaks and string them together until they didn't seem broken at all.

THE DJ OF ALL DJS

I once heard a song by Pink called "God Is a DJ." I thought the idea of God in front of two turntables, crates filled with every song ever written in all of time, spinning, mixing, scratching, was kind of cool. I imagined maybe that's what heaven was like, a big dance party where God is flipping the same fingers that birthed creation across the crossfade, scratching "Holy holy holy" in the pocket while the angels break bad in these fresh clean kicks that look like Adidas but are oh-so-much better.

Pink's metaphor was cool until I dug into it, realizing if God is the DJ and my life is the dance floor, then he is in constant control of the songs that play. Sometimes right as I'm getting into the groove of a particular tune, Mr. DJ of All DJs switches the cut on me, forcing me to find a completely new rhythm to dance to.

I began my relationship with Jesus at twelve years old. Thankfully, I was choosing a life of love, grace, peace, joy and purpose. Unfortunately, I also accepted a safe Christianity that involved more boredom than risk, more cliché than creativity, more of a narrow mind than an open one. By the time I reached my mid-twenties I was swiftly arriving at disillusionment. I took a long, hard look at this Jesus I had learned about at youth camp, this Jesus who required I promise my virginity and vocation away to him indefinitely—this Christ who would not let me be like everybody else.

The closer I get to him the more I want Jesus to show me his turntables, teach me how to do a dance that requires more guts than my boring two-step. Maybe he's been waiting for me to get tired of my same old song. It is this journey that has led me here, watching my monotonous break snap in two and therefore learning how to break dance.

This is the tension. If life is a dance floor, the song and dance will constantly change. The question is, Will we stop at nothing to keep dancing, or will we let a change of song we're not fond of push us and our backs to the wall?

GOD, THE UNTOUCHABLE

Every Thelma must have a Louise, and every B-girl must have another B-girl to share her love of hip hop with. For me, it is my friend Kimberly. We have stood on the side of stage to watch MC Lyte rock the house, Slick Rick and Doug E. Fresh perform "The Show," and the Juice Crew reunite. We wear our B-girl sneakers and dance until our feet hurt.

I decided to try an idea from the movie *Bucket List* and make a list of DJs I wanted to see before I died. Thankfully I have been able to experience three of these so far, and who else would be a better B-girl partner than Kimberly?

DJ BUCKET LIST (IN NO PARTICULAR ORDER)

1. Jazzy Jeff
2. Questlove
3. Pete Rock
4. Biz Markie
5. Spinderella
6. Red Alert
7. Grandmaster Flash
8. D-Nice

Rapper Common was performing a free show in Atlanta featuring DJ Jazzy Jeff. One of hip hop's premier DJs and producers, Jeff was world-renowned before he became famous for being thrown out of Uncle Phil's house on the *Fresh Prince of Bel Air*. When we arrived at the concert, he was situated in a sound booth perched near the ceiling. I couldn't see the kind of turntables Jazzy Jeff was rocking, whether he was using a computer or if he was still spinning vinyl, couldn't look at him crossfade. But I could feel the beats he was spinning in my chest. He was mixing the kind of music where your arms don't ask your permission but voluntarily end up in the air bouncing to the downbeat. He was spinning the songs I had listened to on my Discman until the CD skipped, the tunes I pressed "Record" and "Play" to capture from the radio, the R&B I remember dancing to at my high school homecoming. He didn't just play my song. He played my decade. Half the fun was guessing where he was going next with his playlist.

No matter what faith we ascribe to (or refuse to ascribe to), we are all in some way searching for God, longing for love, desperate for peace, hoping that hope is more than a wish. At first I thought of God as far away, white, bald, with a long beard that rivaled Rapunzel's hair. He didn't talk, just sort of nodded or raised three fingers like many paintings depict him. I always pictured him sitting on a bunch of clouds: clean, righteous and old. Nothing like me. I felt like I'd never meet his standard. Maybe that was only for saints or nuns or kids who got perfect attendance in elementary school.

Sometimes God, like DJ Jazzy Jeff's setup, seems perched up high, unreachable, untouchable, disconnected, because we can't see what he's doing or if he cares. God is in fact reachable, touchable, connected. He is also holy, which means he is not saddled with the imperfection of humanity. He is always righteous, always right, always loving, always King, always perfect and to our human understanding he will always be mysterious.

When we accept this, we learn the mystery of faith—that although our God is higher and greater than all of his creation, he is also intimately acquainted with his creation. Whether or not we can see his fingers do the mixing, he is constantly crafting a rhythm to help us live our lives more like him.

OFF THE WALL

Some mornings
I sit before him
Pad in hand
Pen in grip
And ask what does he want me to write?
How does he want me to live my life?
All I've got is pages and faith
But I believe
I believe he'll come through like he always does
Breaking down the walls of Jericho
In the land of Canaan and in our souls
AMENA BROWN, *INCONVENIENT SAVIOR*

I returned to MJQ to see DJ Questlove, famed drummer of hip-hop band The Roots. The band had a tour stop in Atlanta, and sometimes when The Roots are on tour Questlove DJs at local spots. Kimberly and I got there early and stood next to the DJ booth, but the wall was so high I had to hold my camera up at arm's length to take a picture.

I spent the rest of the night trading time between dancing and standing on the balls of my feet to sneak a peek at watching

Questlove work. But I could only catch a glimpse of his Afro and Afro pick. I stood close to him but not close enough to know or understand what he was doing or how he was going to make it work. My experiences with Questlove and God were the same: there was a wall between us.

Watching Questlove reminded me of all the times I thought I was doing good at being good and then failed, messed up, disappointed myself or God or other people. All of the times when I didn't get the job, didn't get into grad school, lost someone I loved, suffered a breakup, went broke, and felt alone and like God couldn't possibly understand or care.

Sometimes it can feel like there is this wall between God and me, this tension where I treat him like a distant roommate who I live with but don't have to speak to, where I just want to do my own thing without having to consider him.

Whenever I feel far from God, it is never that he has walked away, become preoccupied or is completely disgusted with me. It is most likely that I have allowed my pride, unforgiveness, anger, lies, unbelief or sin to plant my feet in a vicious moonwalk that slowly and seductively dances me away from him.

I could only get so close to the DJ booth, but there's always something we can do to get closer to God. "Come near to God and he will come near to you" (James 4:8). Maybe it starts with being honest enough with him to admit we don't want to do what it takes to be closer to him and ask for his help. Maybe it starts with forgiving someone, letting go of a grudge. Maybe it means telling him we're hurt, angry, disappointed. He's waiting for us to dismantle our walls and let him mend us, in the same way a DJ can connect the beat and tone of two records.

JESUS ON THE WHEELS OF STEEL

Kimberly and I went to hear Pete Rock DJ in a warehouse of a room, with nothing on stage but him and his turntables. We stood feet away from him and watched him work, shuffling beats, melody, lyrics and mixing. He looked as if it didn't so much matter to him that we were there. He looked like he was enjoying DJing the way he had the first time he'd ever set up turntables in his room.

When God DJs, I bet it's like when I saw Pete Rock, no barriers, no distance, just an open invitation to watch him work. Jesus came here to show us his turntables, to play us tunes from God's music. And I'm not just talking about the genre of music you hear on your local Christian radio station. I'm talking about God's rhythm, God's melody, the one he's constantly trying to get us to turn down the noise of our lives and listen to. This is what it meant for Jesus to come to earth and walk here as a human being. He wanted to show us how to listen, how to live.

If I can translate the story of Jesus into hip hop, I'd say he's a DJ and—here's the amazing part—he's still spinning. He's got this eternal song that's playing through all these situations in our lives. When we get to heaven we'll recognize it. By coming down to earth, showing us how to live and by dying and rising from the dead, Jesus became the reason none of us have to approach God from far away or behind a wall anymore.

If God is a DJ, we are all songs. Not only do we all have a rhythm, but we've also all had breaks: disappointments, pain, loss, successes, failures. DJing hinges on two things: the break and the timing. God orchestrates both extremely well. He takes every break you've ever experienced and mixes it with the tune of hope and the rhythm of his sovereignty to create the beautiful mix of story that will be your life.

Sometimes a break, beat or hook by itself won't make much sense, but when a DJ gets hold of it, he can take those broken pieces and make a new song out of them. Each of our life stories and experiences are like tunes, and Jesus has this amazing way of connecting stories, beats, people and rhythms. We look up, and he's blended, mixed, matched and mastered life—our background, family, mistakes, relationships, calling, mercy and grace—with the crossfader of a Savior. It is at his cross that our sins fade, and we stand righteous behind the power of his name.

Romans 8:28 says, "And we know that in all things God works for the good of those who love him, who have been called according to his purpose." That's proof that God is a DJ.

On the dance floor, the DJ saves us from boredom and gives us a tune to dance to. But God as DJ does far more: he saves our lives from sin, selfishness and hopelessness, and he gives our lives new purpose.

I want to break bad with the angels. I want to rhyme "Holy, holy, holy" over the sickest drumbeat heaven's drummers can muster. I want to learn to do a mean two-step to whatever cool tune the DJ of all DJs is putting down. And that is a tune worth listening to.

BREAKING RHYTHM

In the film *I'm Gonna Git You Sucka,* John Slade suggested that "every hero needs a theme song." What is your theme song? Why?

Go to an event where you can watch a good DJ at work. Reflect on the connections you make between the DJ's work and God's work in your life.

Read Romans 8:28. How is God DJing in your life right now?

FIVE

BROKEN HEART

The emotions of love can be sweet
With the rush and crash of sugar and sea
Carry you to a mountain's peak
And drop you swift from the top of the Empire State building
Until you feel like your face is imprinted in a New York City sidewalk

AMENA BROWN, *LESSONS LEARNED*

I've heard people pray for God to break their hearts; I've even prayed that prayer myself without giving it much thought. Maybe because I'd never had a broken heart before.

Always a late bloomer, I fell swiftly in love for the first time at age twenty-seven, and shortly after I turned twenty-eight I suffered my first romantic heartbreak. I'll call him Coen, for all the Coen brothers' movies I endured due to my serious crush on him. Our time dating had been fun, but wrought with the tension that happens between two people when they want two different things out of life and out of their relationship.

One night Coen sent me a text asking if I'd meet him for dinner. He wanted to talk. Studies show that phrases like "We need to talk" are not followed by a marriage proposal or grandiose professions of love. I was getting dumped.

We met at the restaurant, ordered some food and made small talk for a while. Then Coen looked into my eyes and told me he was walking away from what I had come to believe was "us."

Had he been a doctor, he might as well have written me a prescription: "Take this broken heart, and don't call me in the morning."

I took it well—only because I had been crying my eyes out for two days prior, preparing my heart for the break. We somehow finished our meals while I expressed my bleeding heart and how much he meant to me, and he repeated, "I never meant to hurt you."

Breaking up sucks, but getting dumped is the worst. When you are the dumper, you walk away from a breakup conversation hurting, but feeling a sense of relief. When you are the dumpee, on the other hand, you leave with embarrassment, hoping your stabbed heart will wait to bleed until you are in the privacy of your own bedroom closet, praying your ego will retain its elasticity until you are alone with the thoughts of what must be wrong with you to make you so unlovable.

Being dumped is a grieving process. For the first couple of weeks I was in denial, sure he would turn back and forget this whole breaking-up idea. The next two weeks I was angry that he took it upon himself to end something that I hoped would turn out to be good. And then it finally settled in. The man I loved didn't want me anymore, and there was nothing I could do to change it.

All by Myself

It is a truth universally acknowledged that when one part of your life starts going okay, another falls spectacularly to pieces.

BRIDGET JONES, IN *BRIDGET JONES'S DIARY*

Like many single women, I'd watched *Bridget Jones's Diary*, chuckled and giggled at the scene where she's smoking cigarettes and downing ice cream while listening to what has to be the worst song to keep on repeat when you're depressed: Celine Dion's "All by Myself." This scene is worth the chuckle and the giggle—until you become your own sad, depressed version of Bridget Jones: eating anything you can, a la mode, swearing off Alicia Keys, Luther Vandross and Prince for their ridiculous love songs, crying your eyes out until your face swells and won't return to its normal size, sending every call to voicemail and answering via text just so friends know you're alive and to keep them off your doorstep. Broken hearts are horrible, and once I'd experienced one for myself I questioned whether I'd ever ask God to break my heart again.

During the first few weeks, I attempted to move on. I tried to ignore how down I was feeling, hoping I could dress well enough and put on enough make-up to dress up how sad I was. It didn't work. Sometimes the pull of being hurt and disappointed is too strong to mentally move on, emotions just aren't that logical.

I missed Coen. Wondered how he was getting on without me. Couldn't resist my urge to contact him so I called him. He didn't answer but sent me a text: "I'm out at an event. What's up?"

No smiley face. No exclamation. No indication he was excited to hear from me. More indication that I was an interruption. It made me wonder if that's what I had been all this time. I sat alone on the same couch where we'd laughed and watched movies, and finally cried.

That breakup taught me that crying is not meant to be productive—at least not in a task-oriented, to-do-list kind of way. For the first time in my life I gave myself permission to hurt, cry and be disappointed, to feel those negative emotions, to accept that there was nothing I could do to change what happened.

I used to think letting go was final. You make this decision that you're through with something or someone, and you are through. And you move on. And it doesn't hurt anymore. And eventually you can be friends with the person and shoot the breeze and act like this moment that changed things never happened.

The fact that letting go is a process surprised me. I know logically I could gather that it would be true, but having to go through it myself was a totally different experience. There's nothing enjoyable about a broken heart. There's nothing enjoyable about pain no matter how it comes to us, but it is one of life's greatest teachers. If we face it instead of avoiding it, it can help us to grow as individuals and to grow closer to God.

I described it this way in my diary:

I know that God's here. And I know there's something to learn here. And I'm coming to the point of finally admitting that I don't know what that lesson is. That all my processing can't figure that out. That there is no way to fix this. That this isn't happening so it can be fixed. That in a way this is teaching me to trust in a way I don't think I ever learned before.

Help me Jesus to just take it one moment at a time. Help me not to worry about tomorrow or the next day or next year or my next relationship or when this will all be over. Help me to hold your hand and walk with you one step at a time. I read this morning that "you've kept track of my every toss and turn through the sleepless nights, each tear entered in your ledger, each ache written in your book" (Psalm 56:8, *The Message*). And I believe that's true.

It may be hard to imagine but, even when our hearts are broken, God is with us. The Bible offers this solace: "The LORD is close to the brokenhearted and saves those who are crushed in spirit" (Psalm 34:18). God is not just a God who is there with you in good times. He is a God who is there with you all the time. As

painful as it is to walk through, God uses our broken hearts to
teach us something.

A Broken Heart Gives You Compassion

A broken heart breaks our rhythm with a screeching stop. Maybe,
like me, you experienced a breakup or the end of a relationship,
maybe you've experienced the death of someone you love, maybe
you've lost a job, career or opportunity with no hope, it seems, of
going forward. One of the hardest things about a broken heart is
the helpless feeling that you can't change what happened. You
can't escape or avoid it. The only way to heal is to walk through it
until you find yourself on the other side.

A broken heart reminds us that we're human. You would think
with all of our imperfections that we wouldn't need much reminding
of this, but being human isn't just to remind us that we're irrepa-
rably flawed. Our humanity reminds us that we exist in this world
with other human beings. No matter how different our culture,
background, economic status, family structure or appearance, our
humanity is what we all have in common. At some point, we all cry
when it hurts and get angry when we've been mistreated.

I've had moments when I met someone at a party, at a conference or through a friend of a friend. We didn't know each other's
life story, didn't grow up together, had no history, but we found
common ground in the things we had survived or were in the
process of surviving.

This means a broken heart is never wasted. When you've had a
broken heart, you know the damage that words like "Just get over
it" can do. This is a chance to be more human and less holier-than-
thou. When we hurt, when we suffer, the greatest thing we can do
for other people is let them know they are not alone after all.

This is part of what's amazing about Jesus: part of why he put
on human skin is so he could demonstrate we're not alone. When

he says he's with us, those aren't empty words; he means he has experienced the depth of everything that has and ever will hurt us. If we want to follow Jesus' rhythm we will be a glimpse of his love for others by taking our broken heart experiences and giving them hope.

HEALING AND HOPE

God can show us more of who he is when we agree that we're frail and weak. This is the difference between allowing ourselves to experience sad emotions and wallowing there. To experience these emotions is to be real; to run to God with these emotions is part of what keeps us from staying stuck there.

Most of the time, if not all of the time, the moments and experiences in life that break us take us to the bottom and end of ourselves. As devastating as that can be, it also gives us hope that there is something better.

God is a fascinating Artist. He is the DJ who scratches and mixes our "breaks" to match the rhythm of his love. He is the Master of montage and collage, creating fantastic patchwork out of every moment we experience. Where your heart, relationships, dreams and life have been broken, God hands are strong for the mending.

In the plot of my life story, Coen wasn't meant to be the leading man. God had planned all along that Matt, who is now my husband, would be that leading man. Although my heart ached at the time to see my relationship with Coen end, I'm glad it did, knowing now what a wonderful plot twist my love life was going to take.

There were years between that hurtful ending and my new beginning with Matt. In that in-between time, I had to ask myself a lot of hard questions. Did I follow God because of what he could do for me? Or did I follow him because I truly believed in my heart, not just in my head, that he is good and his character allows him to be nothing else?

He didn't promise me a replacement for my broken relationship so that my ego could feel justified. He didn't promise us we would never lose, never fail. He did not say he would be a genie to grant all of our wishes. He promised us his love would never fail. He wants to be our Father, our Leader, our Redeemer. He wants to teach us that he is enough. This is the beginning of our healing. This is the center of our hope.

Sometimes, later in our journey, we understand how a broken heart helped us. Sometimes that broken heart never quite makes sense. This is the mystery of God and his plans. We don't always have the answers; we don't always understand.

Enduring a broken heart isn't just about the exchange or the fix. God doesn't wait for the replacement of what was lost to heal what's broken. The challenging part about a broken heart is that we don't get to choose how God mends us. Sometimes we just don't want to be hurt and disappointed anymore. This is the beauty and challenge of faith. We can come to a place where we believe that even when we hurt, even when we don't understand, that a perfect God is watching over us, looking out for us, writing our story, composing the notes that make up the song we will live.

Loving and being loved isn't safe. It's risky, messy, beautiful and vulnerable. Love is no sanctioned, private school, junior high dance with a stern teacher keeping everyone dancing five feet apart. Love doesn't keep its distance, waiting for us to reach perfection. God is love and he wants to step in my dirt with me. He wants me to understand that love can't be had while holding someone at arm's length.

Sometimes the hardest thing for us is not loving God but letting God love us. His love wants to hold us close, and in his love we are safer than in any fortress we could ever build to protect ourselves. Seeing God's love this way taught me a profound lesson about accepting instead of being repulsed by other people's dirt. When the occasion presented itself I would be asked to love people close. I had to accept that they might leave, would probably disappoint and would never be perfect, because, like me, they are human. They could be loved and so could I because God had given me the power. On many occasions I would be forced to choose between my sanitized safety and true love. True love with its risky business is always better, always worth it.

We need God and we need love. If this life with God were safe, we'd never have a need to come to him. We'd have it all under control—and that is pretty boring. No fantastic plotlines to that story.

Jesus is our example. Throughout the Gospels Jesus' life was constantly threatened and in danger. Jesus also wasn't safe from being hurt by those closest to him as he was betrayed by one of his own disciples. In his most trying time, during the trial before his crucifixion, his followers fled and ran. Jesus put his life and heart at risk, and if we are to do greater things than these, our lives will be at risk too.

BROKEN HEARTS FOR THE WORLD

Outside of our own personal circumstances there is a world of hurting people whose situations should break our hearts. This is probably the origin of those prayers I heard people pray. It can be so easy to go about our day and our lives solely concerned with ourselves, when there are people around us hurting and in need every day.

Whether you go to another country or serve in your neighborhood, what's most important is that you live a life that's about more than your own. Allow yourself to get close enough to someone, or to an injustice or cause, that it could break your heart. Possibly in the process of taking that risk, you can help to mend broken hearts and prevent some hearts from being broken in the first place.

Maybe to some degree we're supposed to keep a broken heart.

Because to the extent we don't we're not exemplifying the life Jesus lived, as that is what it really means to be a Christian. It's not just where you go to church on Sunday, or if you wear T-shirts with scriptures on them; being a Christian means being like Jesus. He was selfless, and as much as I'd like to excuse myself because I'm tired, spent, traveling, whatever, if I'm going to be like him I have to live like the world doesn't revolve around me. And get this: The world does literally revolve around Jesus. He's God! But even he came to earth to serve others and put their needs before his own.

Our challenge is not just to say these things because they sound good and then go on watching our favorite TV shows every night as usual. Our challenge is to find people in need and serve them. Not because it makes us feel better. Not because we're better than them. Truth is, we're all in need. We learn when we serve with hearts that want to learn, listen and understand. Serving others keeps our hearts broken in the best way.

Breaking Rhythm

- How has God mended your heart in the past? How do you notice him mending you lately?

- What people in your life might need your compassion right now?

- What is one way you can serve others who are broken or in need?

SIX

BREAK DANCING

He puts his hand in the small of my back
Two fingers pressed into the center of my palm
Pulls me close and steps with his left
My right
I focus on his eyes and try to ignore my feet
as they clumsily count 1, 2, 3
I'm trying to trust him
He knows this dance better than me

AMENA BROWN, *DANCE WITH HIM*

*E*arly in my life I discovered I had a slight case of chorophobia, fear of dancing. All cultures, ancient and modern, make a practice of dancing—in formal settings from religious ceremonies, worship, weddings and mating rituals to informal settings at house parties, on cardboard in front of a DJ table, and in the privacy of our own homes in our pajamas to our favorite song. Most of us at some point have found ourselves afraid to boogie because of stage fright, two left feet, a complicated beat or the thought of completely embarrassing ourselves.

When I was seven years old, my dad had just returned to the

United States from being stationed in Okinawa, Japan, in the military. As a surprise, he flew in to his and my mom's hometown, where I'd been living with my grandma. There was a Brownie Girl Scouts talent show coming up, and I was at the beginning of what would be a few years' fascination with Janet Jackson's music. I had her third album, *Control,* on cassette. I chose "What Have You Done for Me Lately" as the soundtrack to my dance routine. Prior to my dad's arrival I had planned some sassy seven-year-old dance moves to dazzle my fellow Brownie sisters.

I stood in front of my grandma's clunky silver sound system, complete with glasstic-cover record player and a cassette deck with large picture buttons for rewind, forward, play/pause and stop. My dad was on the couch reading the paper. I turned the song on and was embarrassed to tears. I couldn't let loose and dance in front of my dad. I had suddenly caught a terrible case of discomfort, shyness and withdrawal.

My dad put his arms around my shoulders and asked me what was wrong. I couldn't tell him; I was choked by a swell of emotions. "You don't want to do the talent show? You don't have to," he said. I nodded and gave myself permission to forget my hard-earned dance moves.

I'm still a lot like my seven-year-old self. Every time I dance it reminds me of my life and how scared I am to jump out there. Dancing brings out the worst fears in me: fear of looking clumsy, messing up, not having it all together, falling or failing.

Sometimes I live as if I'm standing in front of a session of double-dutch on my elementary school playground. I'm staring at the ropes, trying to find where my own rhythm and the rhythm of the rope intersect; scared I'll ruin the whole thing if I jump in on the wrong beat. The two girls turning rope are popping gum, twisting their pigtails, blowing bubbles, doing cheers and never missing a beat with their arms swinging the rope to its proper snatch as it hits the ground, creating its own percussive sound. All I can do is jump in, right? Jump in and try. These pigtail girls are professional. They can probably pop gum, tie their shoes, tell a tale and swing that rope in proper time. They won't be ruined if I jump in all wrong. They'll chew a fresh piece of gum and start over, which is all I can ask myself to do.

As I got older, I slowly grew out of my fear of grooving in public. From break dance crews, party scenes in music videos, Spike Lee's *School Daze* step routines to Michael and Janet Jackson's intricate choreography, I was learning you didn't have to get down alone.

DANCE WITH ME

I went to my first school dance when I was eleven years old, in sixth grade. Picture it: my hair in curly braids with extensions, ponytail up and to the side, with some braids hanging down in the back. Oversized purple Gap sweater, floral-print pants, and a pair of British Knights. It was my first year of junior high. In a matter of a year I went from snacks and a cubbyhole to wood shop and a locker, from thinking boys were gross to finding them slightly cute and very interesting.

My mom dropped me off at school that night. Our cafeteria had been transformed into a dance floor, with requisite cheesy disco lighting and DJ. The somewhat-cute-but-still-kind-of-gross boys were on one side of the room and all of us girls were on the other side, chewing gum, twirling hair, giggling, not knowing why all of a sudden gross boys were making our hearts beat so fast. The only thing that interrupted the awkwardness was music.

It was 1991, the year of the Teenage Mutant Ninja Turtles, the Super Soaker and the Fly Girls from *In Living Color.* Yeah, I wanted to be one of them. They wore baggy pants and fly boots and danced to all the latest hits—and they looked cute doing it. Music videos and movies taught us all the latest footwork. *School Daze* had introduced "Da Butt," a song with a go-go beat that invited you to shake your derrière any way you felt like it.

This, plus the "Hammer" dance I practiced in my living room while watching MTV and BET, made for a great evening. This was when dancing until you were sweating was cool. You could groove by yourself or with your crew. My prepubescent friends and I did "Da Butt," "the MC Hammer" and "the Roger Rabbit" all night long. Hip hop music led me to the dance floor and wrapped its beat around my waist. It taught me I could freestyle a little and find my own rhythm.

In high school I went to my first house party. By now it was the late 1990s. We weren't in junior high anymore. We were moving away from the dance crews entertaining the party and getting more interested in guys and girls dancing together. The boys were outrageously cute, and any thought of them being gross had left my mind years ago. Boys and girls were swaying together to the music instead of leaning on the walls on opposite sides of the room.

My friend Latanya was turning sixteen, and her parents loved her enough to let twenty or so teenagers invade their home for a few hours. The adults were downstairs, watching TV, making food and playing cards. A guest room upstairs had been converted into the dance floor, complete with boom box and strobe light. So far high school had been good to me. I had traded in my Coke-bottle glasses for contacts, abandoned my ponytail for a shorter curl-layered haircut.

A young man—I'll call him Dalvin—was one of the smoothest guys and best dancers in our high school. He showed up at the party in a fresh white T-shirt, crisp jeans and clean sneakers. I immediately reverted to my junior high ways and leaned against the wall with the other nervous girls. A slow song came on by the

R&B group Jodeci. I turned my head to talk to the girl next to me, and when I turned back to face forward, Dalvin was standing in front of me.

"Would you like to dance?" he asked, even though one of his hands was already on my waist.

He led me to the center of the room and pulled me close. All sorts of sirens and alarms and shouts of joy galloped between my thoughts and my skin. I heard all my grandmother's warnings in my head about not being fast, about not getting close to a boy, about not getting pregnant, about not wearing red lipstick, about not wearing my clothes too tight. But I couldn't think very clearly. I was dancing chest-to-chest and hip-to-pelvis with a boy—a handsome, older, slick-talking boy.

When the song was over, he slowly let go of my waist and hands until he was walking all the way across the room. A fast song came on, and soon after that my mom came to get me. When I got home that night and shut my bedroom door, I could still smell Dalvin's Cool Water cologne on my shirt.

I learned then that dance could be innocent and fun, but it could also be steamy and feel dangerous, that maybe I was right to have been afraid in the first place. By the time I got to college, I gave up dancing hip-to-pelvis, refused to go to the club or to date—not because I was by any means holy but mostly because I was afraid. I felt pretty certain that if I went to a club I would love it way too much to stop going three days a week; I would never do my schoolwork. So I gave up on dancing altogether, outside of a safe two-step at church and school functions.

FAS-SUH-NAY-SHUN

I never danced formally until my sophomore year of college when, at my mother's behest, I agreed to be a debutante. My friend Eric agreed to be my escort.

An elderly woman with a salt-and-pepper Farrah Fawcett hairdo that stuck to her head like a helmet taught us to waltz. We were dancing to "Fascination," a song I would be happy never to hear again. Each time she instructed us on the count she would say, "Fas-suh-nay-shun I know, two, three." Eric and I would laugh, our hands awkwardly placed on shoulder and at waist, trying not to look at our feet.

My dad flew in on the weekend of the event, so he did not have the luxury of weeks of "Fas-suh-nay-shun I know, two, three." He had to endure the waltz crash course, complete with turns and bow. On day two of our lesson, he said, "Did you know that when we're turning, you squeeze my shoulder and turn it in the direction of the way you think we're supposed to be going?"

"What?!" I said, aghast, then stared at my death grip on his shoulder, my fingerprints burning through his sweater. That was my first lesson that I may have learned how to waltz but didn't know how to follow.

In a formal dance, the man is the lead. He controls the turns; he keeps an eye out on the dance floor so that the two of you don't run into other couples. He makes sure you step in your space wisely. In a formal dance, the woman's job is to relax her arms, fingers, back and shoulders, to stand strong and straight but fluid enough to be directed, to keep good rhythm and be ready for any turn. A good male dancer can make a woman who is a novice look like she knows what she's doing, if he leads her well.

Learning how to waltz for my debutante ball made me see for the first time the beauty of the metaphor of Jesus as groom and the church as his bride. If faith is a dance, Jesus is always the lead. He controls the turns; he teaches us to turn in the space he's given us. This requires us to surrender to him, to trust that he knows what he's doing and where we're going.

Learning How to Follow

i was raised in a house where the men were absent
stolen by death and divorce
leaving only a lonely fedora hanging on old coat rack
and their last names as reminders of where they'd been
i was raised by women who were trained to survive
who couldn't take the time it took to lick wounds
who must be modern Hagars, pack child and past on their back
and travel roads far from home

Amena Brown, *House Full of Women*

It's one thing to swing to the bass beat of your own DJ; it's something altogether different to share your rhythm with someone else, letting them lead the turns. I come from a line of strong women who for better or worse had not had much opportunity in their lives to be led. My grandma and my mom were both single parents most of their lives, which means that whether they wanted to or not, they didn't have the luxury of submitting to a man as head of the household. They were mom, coach, encourager, breadwinner and hard worker.

I learned from these women how to lead, how to make things happen for myself and how not to depend too heavily on anyone in case disappointment lurked in the shadows of the future. This made me a leader. I'm still learning how to follow.

Having a relationship with Jesus presses all of my "Do not want to be vulnerable" buttons. Knowing him requires learning to follow him, depend on him, surrender to him, submit to him, trust that he knows better than I do and believe that he knows what's best for me even when I can't see my way.

God and I, from Father to daughter, are still having the same moment I had in my heart when I was learning to dance with my dad. It's that moment when I try to take care of things myself, refusing to trust God or his intentions, assuming he is just too busy for me, doesn't find my requests important, has other things he'd rather attend to. Not true.

I think I'm afraid of being let down, discovering this whole thing between me and God is a farce, that he really doesn't love me like he says he does, that he views my incessant prayers as whining and can't wait for me to grow up, stop crying and stand on my own two feet. Woman up. I think it hurts God's heart when I get stuck believing this—because he loves me and he's never too busy for anyone he loves. He wants me to see him as he really is, not for who my hurtful experiences have made him out to be. It hurts his heart because he knows when I believe that God who is love doesn't really love me, I will continue to build my life on something that just isn't true. Where in the world did I get that thinking? Not from the God who wants me to cast all my cares at his feet. Not from the God who knows my intimate details down to the follicles of my hair.

Eric, my dad and I survived the waltz, the turns and bows, and an evening in dresses and tuxedos that were too tight and shoes that hurt our feet. After that, dance and I grew apart again, until a couple of years ago when I needed an intervention.

DANCE LESSONS

After my relationship with Coen ended, I spent weeks avoiding most personal contact, crying off and on, and wearing sweatpants, nursing my broken heart. Somewhere around the three-month mark the haze started to break. I had been planning to schedule salsa classes for the two of us, but since I'd always wanted to learn formally, I decided to take lessons by myself. Dance lessons forced me to get out of the house, and it turned out they would teach me more than steps and choreography.

———∞———

My heart has been hurt before
I have been burned before
Loved and endured loss before
I am in no mood for a dance
No mood to be romanced
I have become a grace cynic and love's worst critic
He sends me invitations every day and I have yet to RSVP
But he doesn't mind me
Keeps pursuing and taking steps in spite of me
AMENA BROWN, *DANCE WITH HIM*

———∞———

When I walked into Academy Ballroom I was a bit skeptical. The room was filled with mostly older people doing what looked to be the waltz. I was under the impression that I was coming to a salsa party, so I was definitely expecting something louder, faster and more hip. Since I was already there I decided to take a seat and take a look. I had to give it to them: they made dancing look effortless and classic.

It turns out I had arrived on the wrong night if I was looking for a salsa party. This was the ballroom's Grand Party, a night for dance students and anyone else interested to come together and shimmy however the music led.

I wasn't seated long and didn't have much time to ponder whether or not I should stay before an older gentleman asked me to dance. He was not put off by my first-time-ness. He taught me to tango.

It's amazing how hard it is to learn something when you think you know it already. I've always had a good sense of rhythm, so I figured learning to tango would be easy. But I came to realize that although I knew how to dance, I didn't know *this* dance and I would fare much better to listen, learn and watch an instructor or someone who knew better than I did. The first steps of any dance are clumsy. No one, even the most talented dancer, wakes up with perfect, unpracticed steps. Any perfection you think you see came from hours of behind-the-scenes stumbling.

Breaking rhythm is no different. Learning how to dance, by its nature, is breaking rhythm. My feet had to learn how to stay in a line. I had to learn how to move from the waist without the involvement of my shoulders. I had to unlearn some of my hip hop, grooving ways, had to dismiss my ideas of a dance crew and grooving solo and had to learn how to stay in step with a partner. I had to learn how to stand up and walk again after it felt like life and love knocked me down. I had to unlearn some of what I thought it meant to be loved. I had to learn that living is really a balance of learning to groove to any rhythm that comes and not being afraid to freestyle a step of your own.

The whole night when any of the gentlemen would extend their hand to dance with me I found myself saying, "I'm still learning, be patient with me." Some were, and in their patience they taught me a few steps I wouldn't have known had I never danced with them. Some were good dancers but not good teachers. Some were learning just like me so we fumbled and danced all over each other's feet, laughing and enjoying all the mistakes we made. Before the night ended, I had learned the basic steps to the tango, rumba, waltz, swing, foxtrot and salsa.

A GOOD KIND OF TENSION

He wants me to put my hand in his, close my eyes
And trust him
With my life, my heart

> *With worry and I'm so scared*
> *With hurt, worth and unworthy*
> *With loving and unlovable*
> AMENA BROWN, *DANCE WITH HIM*

After this, I took a salsa class. From afar salsa looks so free-wheeling, so easy, like something I could just make up off the top of my head and do really well. Quite the contrary. Salsa has steps and turns that can be simple or grow complicated, and it requires a specific rhythm, small steps and making those steps in a straight line.

My salsa instructor was about five feet tall. I am over six feet tall with heels on. Although I am mostly a sneakers-and-flip-flops girl, salsa requires wearing heels—no rubber soles allowed. Salsa is built on extravagant turns, and rubber soles make those turns extra awkward. I bought a pair of low heels and was ready for class.

I was one of only a couple of single people taking the class. Most of my classmates were couples, some about to get married and learning the steps for their wedding receptions, some married awhile and wanting to add some *caliente* to their relationship. Our instructor paired us off and taught the basic step to the ladies first, right foot back and then to the middle, left foot front. We worked through this slowly until we were all on the same beat. Then he taught the men their lead steps, opposite of ours, left foot front then to the middle, right foot back.

"Okay, you all are doing good. Now, gentlemen, raise your right hand. Place it lightly on the waist of your partner. Take your left hand and hold the palm of your partner's hand between your thumb and your pointer finger and middle finger. Don't squeeze her hand or her waist to death. Try your steps now."

He counted off. Some of us did okay. Most of us stepped on each other's toes. The instructor came and stood in front me so he could demonstrate the lead.

"Relax your shoulders," he said. "Your shoulders and torso should not control your movement at all. Movement is controlled from your waist down." He put his right hand on my waist and squeezed the palm of my hand lightly between his thumb and two fingers.

"Let me explain something to you all about salsa. It requires tension between you and your partner—a good kind of tension."

He took his left hand and pushed my right arm lightly which fell to my side. "Too weak," he said and took my hand. "Now tighten your arm."

I did, and this time when he tried to push it, it didn't move at all. "Too tight," he said and took my hand. "Now, keep your arm firm, but relaxed. Don't strain."

I did.

"Now, I will show you all the basic step."

He counted off, and we did the basic step together. He turned me, and then held my hand while he did a turn himself. He turned me until we were only connected by one hand holding the other, and then he pulled me back into the basic step. While he did these turns he explained, "In order for this dance to work, the partners must have a slight tension between them—some push and some pull. Not enough tension, and it will feel like you are dancing with a wet noodle. Too much tension, and each step will feel forced. The right amount of tension and the dance will work beautifully."

He turned on the music, and we practiced our newly learned steps in real time. I wondered if the tension he talked about was a part of how our will and God's will work together. God gave humans free will so that how he relates to us would not be like having a relationship with a wet noodle or a robot. In turn, it is difficult to follow him when we are determined to have our way despite his way being better, when we are determined that we will not be led. The dance with God works most beautifully when we bring our will to him and let him turn us and teach us new steps as he sees fit.

DANCE WITH SOMEONE WHO
DANCES BETTER THAN YOU

On my first night of learning how to swing dance, the instructor taught us a quick lesson and before I knew it I was gallivanting around the dance floor with plenty of sweaty-palmed partners. After a few songs I took a rest. Silver-haired DJ Alan White, who had been spinning everything swing from Tom Jones to Outkast's *Idlewild*, sauntered over in his cool daddy-o way and said, "I think with some practice you'd be good at this, but let me tell you what your problem is."

Anytime a stone-cold stranger suggests telling you what your problem is you are either really intrigued or completely offended. I decided to hear him out. Maybe he'd save me a trip to my therapist's couch.

"Your problem is, you never dance with anyone who dances better than you. If you did, you'd find yourself dancing better too," he said.

Okay, so yeah, I nearly got offended. And I wondered if we were talking about swing at all or if he had somehow hacked into my journal and read my dating history. There's something to be said for this, why it's easy to stay in a relationship with someone who you know isn't good for you, or who you know won't commit to you: for some reason it seems easier. We learn the most in our relationships when we allow ourselves to be connected to people who challenge us.

Alan proceeded to send all of the good dancers my way, including the instructor. I was nervous. I was stepping all over them and myself. The simple fact that they could challenge me caused me to focus too much on the steps and not enough on the experience and all there was to learn. I noticed that the less I focused on my feet and let the music guide me and my partner lead me, the more I was able to keep time and do the steps. But the minute I would think too hard I'd step too slow, miss a step and apologize profusely all over my partner. I looked at the instructor, who was gliding and leading me across the dance floor as if he could do this dance with his eyes closed, and said to him, "I'm scared dancing with you."

"Of what?" he said and led me into a turn.

"I don't know. You make me nervous."

"You have no reason to be nervous. You're doing great. Just focus on me and the music. Look up at me, not at your feet."

I calmed down, looked into his eyes instead of at my feet and found that my feet knew more of what to do than I thought. And then I thought about God. I whispered in my heart that I wanted to learn to trust him. I wanted to rest my hand on his shoulder and dance, trusting that he wouldn't lead me anywhere to leave me by myself.

GOD, MY DANCE PARTNER

To dance with him, I must give in and give up
Plus the trust it takes to really love
I want to love him unbridled
Believe in him with a faith that is unshakeable like tree roots
centuries deep
Until I learn to follow his time
Take deep breaths; rest my head on his chest and my cares at his feet
That I never fare well as long as I depend on me
AMENA BROWN, *DANCE WITH HIM*

This dance with God involves so much tension. He's the one we're always passing up, looking for something better, something easier, something that costs less sacrifice, less giving up what we want. But God patiently waits. He doesn't throw pity parties for himself. His love doesn't mind taking its time; or rather his love doesn't mind that we are taking the time we could be close to him to search for his substitute. He doesn't even wait with "I told you so." He's holding on for that dance until we come back searching for him. He knows we will. He knows there's no substitute for him. I want to learn to wait like that, to love like that. My love so often involves what I can get, and if I find I can't get anything, I'm out. I fold. I throw my cards in, pack up my toys, pout and refuse to play.

I used to think love was like a chick flick or a really cool episode of *Desperate Housewives*. I used to think love was all dressed up, shiny, sequined, pressed. I realize now that love wears no makeup. Love is beautiful, but love is also plain and simple, unpretentious, determined, fiercely, meekly, humbly strong. Love has working hands, scarred, bruised, veined. Love is unafraid to get its hands dirty.

I hope I learn to love like that. I hope I learn to find my way back to Jesus, waiting for me to dance with him.

By the time I find him I've got tears in my eyes because I'm so sorry. So sorry for searching for him without ever really trying to find him. I don't know if you've seen him, but he's got the most forgiving eyes. He waits. Arms outstretched, waiting as if I'd never walked away and left. I nearly collapse into him, and he holds me up until I find the strength to walk in his love. Now I can rest. Now I can stop trying so hard to search for something he's already given me.

God, my strong and beautiful dance partner in life. I think about how many times I must try to burn my fingerprints into his shoulder when he's not turning the way I'd like him to. Think about how hard it was for me to trust the music and the One leading me to turn me where he might. God is the only one with whom I can truly close my eyes and lay my life bare in his hands and not have to worry that he'll take advantage of me.

Here's the problem: I have been taken advantage of. I have been disappointed. I was raised explicitly and implicitly not to be about that whole lay-your-life-bare-in-anyone's-hands kind of thing. I feel that I have to be in control or the worst may befall me, because it feels like no one has ever protected me and that maybe no one ever will. Sometimes God still catches me with my fingertips burning into his shoulders. I think he smiles, puts his hand over mine and turns me with a surprise dip just to remind me he's got this all under control.

THE DANCE OF SURRENDER

He is a songwriter
Composing notes that hold together eternity
He wants to teach my limbs to sing
He's been waiting to watch me let go of woe and worry
Until my soul sings in that beautiful voice he gave me that I have
somehow come to think is not so beautiful

AMENA BROWN, *DANCE WITH HIM*

———⌘———

Dancing is a lot like surrendering. It's simultaneously letting go and holding on. It's learning new steps, it's following and allowing yourself to be led, it's making up a step when there's no prescribed step in front of you. It's feeling the music, leaning into it. It's taking the focus off of your mistakes and enjoying the moment one goofy step at a time.

I want Jesus to teach me to dance. I'm afraid, but I want him to show me some new steps. I want him to lead me. I want to see him smile and tell me I'm okay even when I step on his feet. I wonder what he smells like—will it rub off on me? I wonder if his scent is fresh or sweet or tender, if it's something I'll swear I've smelled before or if my nostrils will exclaim at every inhalation for some unearthly fragrance lilting toward them with each breath.

I want Jesus to put his arm around my shoulders, except this time I want him to ask me why I'm scared to dance and to stay close to me until I can twirl my best with him, until I can remember he's in every room, that he's felt every feeling. He's a pro at teaching people how to walk on water, on teaching two left feet how to make peace with each other and find a beat they can groove to.

Every day is like returning to this proverbial dance floor, seeing my missteps in the mirror, forcing myself to focus more on God's open arms and less on my two left feet. He's going to show up every day to help me practice, even on the days I forsake it and do other things. He's that consistent and that insistent on loving a flawed human being. And that's what always brings me to tears: that he cares so much, that he loves so much, that I matter that much to him.

I wonder what it would be like to see God dance. I always imagine myself his daughter with cotton-socked feet looking so small on top of his black, wing-tipped Stacey Adams. What? You don't think God would wear Stacey Adams? I imagine that he's got this smile that's more like a place to be than a thing to see. I imagine his rhythm and style are impeccable. I know he's perfect, but he never scoffs at my imperfection. He's a master who never turns down the chance to cut a rug with a novice like me. I think he carries music with him. I think it radiates from his chest, loud and

booming as if he carried a boom box on his shoulder. He inhales
and exhales melody. It comes naturally to him. He's got a song he
wants to teach me to dance to. He wants me to follow his lead. I'm
thinking I'll be learning to do simply that for the rest of my life.

I used to think his dance was some complicated tango I could
never possibly learn to do. I thought following him would mean
falling into the waste bucket of all the other ways I could never
measure up. I'm learning his dance is simple, and I'm learning to
sense his timing instead of trying to guess and count all the
measures. It's not staring at my feet but peering into his eyes and
seeing him face to face. One. Song. At. A. Time.

Conquering Chorophobia

I must conquer my chorophobia, figuratively and literally. I've
found the only way to conquer a fear is to face it, head on. Get
close enough to it that you can feel it breathing your face back like
some special-effects monster. Dancing always reminds me that its
beauty, like life, is not just in mastery. Its beauty is in the sharp-
ening, the repetition, the process, the learning. Little Miss Perfectionist has to give herself the opportunity to have two left feet and
learn to love them.

I discovered that I only like risking when I'm pretty sure I'll
win—and that is not risking at all. I've discovered it doesn't matter
your approach, whether you are a toe-in-the-water, gradual-
immersion kind of person or whether you are a jump-in-the-deep-
end, let-the-strong-current-force-you-to-swim kind of person.
What matters is that you get immersed. What matters is that you
don't give up. No matter how goofy you look, no matter how much
you don't have it together, dance. Learn to freestyle. Learn to feel
the music, embrace the beat and set your rhythm free.

Dance. When you have a bad day, dance. With or without a partner,
dance. Scared? Dance. Every day is a new day to dance. Never lose

patience with yourself. This will help you to have much more patience with everyone else. We're all learning *something*. Quitting never made anyone a good dancer—or good at anything really.

I've spent the rest of my life reclaiming that Brownie talent show moment for myself. I figuratively grab my seven-year-old self and say, "I know you're afraid, I know you're nervous, I know you don't want to be hurt again, I know you don't want to be made a fool of or taken advantage of, I know you want this time to be different. This time you blast that Janet Jackson, shrug those shoulders to the beat and move. Close your eyes and remember that you've got a Heavenly Father who loves to see you dance, lift hands and lose yourself in something way louder than you."

I've got a feeling there's a party going on in heaven with a fantastic DJ, and since I'll have a new body maybe I can wear high heels and my feet will never hurt. In heaven whatever move you do, whether it's a mean salsa or a bouncy knee-jerk thing, it's all to celebrate the One who invented celebration. These earthly dance floors are just practice.

Take his hand
Take a chance
Fingertips in the palm of the One who holds galaxies in hand
Hand on his shoulder
Heart in his hand
His is the song that never ends
In his love sinners become friends
He wants to dance with you until the only song you hear is him

AMENA BROWN, *DANCE WITH HIM*

BREAKING RHYTHM

🖎 Describe your favorite dance moment.

🖎 What is one area in your life where you need to learn to follow? To surrender?

🖎 Take a dance lesson. Jot some notes about what it teaches you about yourself and about God.

SEVEN

BREATHING ROOM

She had cheeks as dark brown as tree trunks.
See the years of courage weaved like the grain of tobacco leaves,
She used to pick, between her fingertips.
These same lips fed me spoonfuls of truth,
thick and hot like stone ground grits.
She knew the blood of Jesus for its pardon and its power,
Called on his name in a way book knowledge cannot teach.

AMENA BROWN, DEAR GRANDMA SUDIE

When I was younger I spent a lot of time with my Grandma Sudie, my southern great-grandmother—tall, lean, graceful with high cheekbones that rose luxuriously like the sun over a range of mountains when she smiled. Her soft, graying hair was styled in the same pageboy press and curl she had worn as a teenager. My grandma worked third shift so from a little after lunch until way past my bedtime I spent most of the day with my Great-grandma Sudie. She was a tall, thin, wonderfully brown woman. She wore slips and stockings and carried a pocketbook. She cooked collard greens and made Kool-Aid, so for the most part I was happy.

She'd ask me to grease her scalp and part her hair, so I'd carve the straightest line my six-year-old hands could manage, dividing her silver hair to the left and to the right. I dipped my fingertips in a jar of White Rose petroleum jelly and slid it down her scalp, separating her hair into four equal parts, and braiding and twisting each one into a bun before she went to sleep.

It was a moist North Carolina summer and the air around Grandma Sudie's house was thick with the scent of the Sunbeam bread bakery around the corner. She soaked, washed, cut and cooked collard greens. I followed her every move, watching her hang clothes on the line and fry fish with cornmeal.

I believed in the power of My Little Pony and, yes, I believed in playing; she believed in God and that you should respect him. I brushed and braided glittered manes and ponytails, while she straightened sheets and tucked hospital corners with a heavy hand. I was full of questions and conversation, and she listened to me as if my words carried more than the weight of my six years.

She knew the scent of rain, and when she smelled a storm coming, she unplugged everything in the house except for the oven and refrigerator, and that was only because she couldn't get back there. There would be no playing, no talking and no whirring. "You be still and be quiet when God is doing his work," she'd say. I may have whined with more than one "But grandma," but she would not be moved. My Little Pony would have to wait.

I told her I hated when it rained. "You never say you hate when God is working," she said.

We would lie in silence until the storm passed, listening to thunder, lightning, water and breathing. I would not learn to appreciate those moments until she was gone.

She and I were three generations apart. I graduated from high school and college, have read countless books on spiritual growth, discipleship, prayer and devotion. After the knowledge I have gained I still long for what she had—this strong knowing that

God was always with her, that her prayers and words mattered to him, that his ears and eyes were attentive to this world, to all these wayward human beings.

Grandma Sudie taught me the power of the pause—a lesson I have the hardest time learning and feel far from mastering. Grandma Sudie didn't graduate from high school, didn't go to college, didn't become a scholar or a theologian, but she had this way of singing to the Lord on her bed at night before she went to sleep. She and the other church mothers held prayer meetings in her living room, where it seemed their petitions and requests rose like fire to God.

My grandma found God in old hymns. She believed he was so present that he heard her prayers immediately with no hesitation. It didn't matter to her whether she was in a church pew, standing in front of her kitchen stove or watching her favorite soap opera. She lived as if she knew God was with her always and everywhere. I want to know God like that. I want to learn to be still when he's doing his work, even though I am sometimes trying so hard to meddle my hands in a job he can do so much better than I can.

THE ART OF INTERLUDE

Some of my favorite songs have what I like to call "breathing room," where the beat breaks down, the singers stop singing, the emcees stop rhyming and all you can hear are the instruments and sounds making music. It's like a moment of musical Selah.

The Roots' album *Undun*, a concept album about a hustler's downfall, ends with four movements—"Redford," "Possibility," "Will to Power" and "Finality," a sharp departure from the rest of the album. "Redford" features Sufjan Stevens soloing, contemplative and melancholy, on piano. "Possibility" is upper register piano with viola, violin and cello. "Will to Power" is spastic piano and drums, while "Finality" is mostly strings with a final and stunning piano chord. It's different: the last four tracks on a hip hop album with no rhyming, no steady beat, no hook and only instruments.

In an age when music sells more by the single than it does by the album, the pleasure of listening to an album all the way through has become lost, but every now and then I push past my inclination to download a single from my favorite music provider and buy the whole CD, download all the tracks and listen. I saved my first listen of The Roots' record for a road trip. As I got to those last four tracks, I felt as if I had finally driven out of the smog-covered city and taken my first breath of air surrounded by trees, flowers and honeybees. It was as if I had been holding my breath and bobbing my head to my own chaos until I finally had a moment when there were no intruding voices and no blaring, annoying beep or beat. There was only the steady count of a bar of music, which included full notes, half notes and rests.

Part of the art of the album was not just the songs but the interludes. The brief pauses in a full work of music provided space for me to reflect, breathe, think, sit, do nothing, prove nothing.

What I learned from my grandma, what she taught me about God, is how much he treasures the interlude—those brief moments in time when we sit still and quiet ourselves to listen.

This reminds me of Psalm 23, which unfortunately in all my Sunday school lessons and youth retreats had become cliché to me, until the first time I took a yoga class.

I took yoga because while I hate working out, I was stressed out with my job at the time and thought yoga might be simultaneously relaxing and rigorous.

In yoga, I was forced for the first time to pay attention to my body as it moved, to focus on how joint, bone and sinew were connected, to notice the pressure in one muscle group and the relief in another as I practiced the various yoga positions. This reminded me of the amazing God who created all joint, bone and sinew with his very fingertips, who breathed life into what would have otherwise been inanimate objects.

At the end of the class when the teacher typically facilitates meditation and clearing the mind, I recited this Scripture I'd learned as a child, wanting to remember the wondrous and creative God I had surrendered my life to.

> The LORD is my shepherd, I lack nothing.
> He makes me lie down in green pastures,
> he leads me beside quiet waters,
> he refreshes my soul. (Psalm 23:1-3)

These verses sound like the opposite of my life. Why doesn't the Scripture say this?

> The Lord is my shepherd, I shall want EVERYTHING.
> He makes me run around like a chicken with my head cut off,
> He leads me to busyness,
> He repeats my chaos.

Something about lying still with no cell phone, no music and just those words in my mind reminded me that even though I fight it and resist, these are things God wants to provide for me. He wants to be my shepherd, my contentment. He wants to be my peace, my healing. A good bit of the time when God brings me to a quiet place, I have been dragged, kicking and screaming.

Silence drastically breaks my rhythm. It's so much easier to avoid what's really going on in our souls, shifting our focus for busyness, for noise, for people, for teeny tiny distractions. Truly coming to know God, to hear his voice, is about bringing our souls to silence, bringing our hearts to a place where they can be alone and quiet with him.

Even in the silence and rest of an interlude, there is still rhythm.

Silence in music has its own rhythm. It lasts for a certain amount of bars. Silence is necessary to complete a song or a poem. The silence or pause allows us to differentiate the refrain from the verse, one stanza from the next. Maybe Selah is God's way of using interlude to let us know when he is about to begin a new refrain or write a new couplet. Maybe he wants to give us a chance to breathe so we can really hear his symphony when it begins.

The Gift of Loneliness

I have approached many times of loneliness in my relationship with Jesus. Many Friday nights passed when no plans panned out. There were simply no quick replacements, no matter how hard I would search. It used to make me angry with God. I thought he kept allowing me to feel lonely to hurt me—as if my loneliness was his punishment, his terrible purgatory, for the fact that I am undesirable and bad company and unloved.

After throwing a few temper tantrums I discovered that punishment was not God's intent at all. It wasn't that God wanted me to hurt or be eternally lonely. It was that in his God way he was using loneliness to show me that I was never alone, that there was this everlasting space that relationship with him was meant to fill. I could run to people, looks or my to do list all I wanted to, but no one and nothing would be as he is.

I was never one of those girls who ascribed to the whole Jesus-is-my-boyfriend idea. It just seemed silly and like a front that church girls used to hide behind even though they really wanted a man, some lips to kiss and a chest to lay their head on. In the break, in the times when God has gotten me away by myself, I've discovered there is something to be said for God being the One who is at all times, on all points, most intimate with me. He knows that although I run to many things to fill the empty feeling in my soul, that void is never satisfied and never will be satisfied until I run to him.

The things it really takes to follow God don't come easy in today's culture. I've always got my phone on me, and half the time I'm carrying my computer. Social networking gives me the voyeuristic pleasure of eavesdropping on other people's lives while posting all of the ignorant, attention-getting things I can muster.

Following God is an ancient practice that sometimes requires us to silence our modernity and unplug to plug in. I am by no means advocating that we all move out to the country, forsaking the Internet and machines for a life of solar-powered everything. I'm not preaching an extreme here. I'm not even preaching. I'm simply telling you what I know: In every relationship, in every ridiculous decision, in our devastation over failure and our constant drive for success, we're just looking for God. And as long as we're busy, noisy and in a hurry, we're not going to find him. We're not going to hear his voice.

You'll feel distracted. You'll hear planes overhead. You'll remember things you forgot to do. You'll think of all the things you've done wrong and see these as reasons why God just doesn't want to hear from you. You'll have to face who you really are when no one is looking or paying attention. You will greet your insecurities face to face. In enough time, you will realize the end of who you are and what you can't do to fix yourself.

This is where God comes in. This is what he's been waiting for: to get you alone so you can see him as he really is. Not for who you've made him out to be, not for the God you've heard preached or sung about, not for the God who disappoints, doesn't love, doesn't care and has better things to do than think about you. I'm talking about you having a moment to spend with the real God, the One who is love and peace and hope and redemption and friendship. He's the one whose bounds of intimacy go so far past what we search for in sex and drugs and drinks and food and all the things we use to try to fill ourselves.

GET SILENT, GET HONEST

When you get quiet and really see yourself as you are, you will find that you start to see God as he is. You will find that your heart will see the words in the Bible so differently. If you want to know God, you can't escape the silence. You can't escape the break.

Maybe you feel like God has been silent too long and you're not going to wait another minute, waste another minute, waiting for a voice that is never going to answer. Maybe your faith in God has gone the way of your belief in the Easter Bunny or in Santa. You just feel too old and jaded to believe that he will act anymore. I'm not going to spit a bunch of clichés at you, give you a Bible reading plan or promise if you cross your legs and listen to a song you'll hear the audible voice of God. I know what it's like to be fed up with God's silence.

I've prayed some frustrated prayers. I've given God ultimatums. I told him the dirt I was sure to get in if he didn't step in and intervene. Fortunately, prayer is not about being proper or following a protocol. Prayer is being honest with God and listening while he is honest with you. Sometimes I have to go to God and tell him that I know what's right, I know what he's asking me to do and I don't want to do it. I tell him I need him to help me want to do what's right. And I have to leave my prayer there.

Having a relationship with God does not always tie up cleanly like some sitcom, where by the time the theme music plays every question and concern has been neatly wrapped into the moral of the story. Following God is an everyday decision. It's not so much how many right things you do or how many wrong things you're sorry for. I'm learning that it's a lot about not letting anything keep you from running back to God—not your own sin, not your busy life. It's about commitment. To follow God is to give your life to him, the whole thing, every part. It's about not quitting when it gets hard or uncomfortable or when you're not going to get your way.

Bare Your (Insert Expletive Here) Soul

I went to my first open mic when I was nineteen. The club was a now defunct hole-in-the-wall spot called Moorepics. It was about as big as a living room. There was incense burning, weed smoking, politicking, flirting and grown people talk, which was a lot for a sheltered, college, church girl to take in. But, in my move to Atlanta, I felt somewhat like an adopted child who had finally found her birth family. I was in a city full of poets, artists, painters, singers, songwriters and musicians. I was irresistibly drawn to any room where they were gathering.

The presentations varied from a poem about rape written from the perspective of the rapist to poems about politics, love, sex and the virtues of weed smoking. A beautiful young woman was next on the mic, her curly hair pinned up in the back with curls dangling in front of her face. The hem of her Greek-styled dress trembled a little, showing us all that she was nervous.

"So I just went through a breakup, and I wrote this poem. I'm going to try and get through this without crying," she said, unfolding the pieces of paper she'd been holding tightly in her fist and started to read.

She didn't succeed in not crying. She stopped several times before finishing the poem that was angry and sad and hurt, just as she was. I wondered how the host would recover from this, how he would prep the audience so that the next poet would actually have their attention, instead of all of us hoping this brokenhearted poet made it through the mess the end of her relationship had left her in.

"Open mic don't have that many rules, but one rule is if you get on this mic, bare your soul. Bare your (insert expletive here) soul."

Poetry and prayer are the same in this way. When you talk with God, bare your soul. He doesn't want your perfunctory, eloquent, well-rehearsed prayers. He doesn't want you to "say your lines." He wants you to bare your soul because he knows how it is anyway. Sometimes we avoid the silence, the moments of Selah, because the longer we avoid them the less we have to deal with how we're really doing, what we really feel and where our life is actually headed.

I often think about the rule of baring your soul when I write. Poetry, like comedy, music and public speaking, is not only about the words, the line and the rhythm. Poetry is also built with space and pause. All art is built this way. Some of the greatest works of art are so beautiful because of the space a painter leaves between a hand and waist, leaf and tree, paintbrush stroke and white canvas space. It is the pause, the line break, the small space after punctuation, the light breath a singer takes between notes, the rest built into a music composition, that makes our eyes, ears, bodies, souls notice what we've just experienced and prepare for what we will experience next.

PAUSE TO LISTEN

In college, I took a poetry workshop from internationally renowned spoken word poet Saul Williams. Each of us had to submit poems to be included in the workshop, and we all brought poems we assumed we'd spend the workshop working through. When we arrived Saul had us introduce ourselves and then pair off.

"For twenty minutes each I want your partners to talk to you about anything and I want you to listen and write. You can write what they say verbatim, you can write what you gather from what they say, you can write something that you were inspired to write as they talk," he said.

So we left the workshop room and walked around campus, timing ourselves talking and listening. When I was the listener, I wrote the phrases, words, notes and body language that stuck out to me about my partner. When it was my turn to talk I couldn't think of anything that felt important enough to say, so I rambled and hoped I wasn't boring my partner to death. When we arrived back in the workshop room Saul asked us to share our experience. Some poets said they'd learned you could find a story anywhere; some said they learned to be more present. Saul nodded.

"We are poets, which means we are scribes. It's our job to scribe history," he said.

We never workshopped our poems. We spent some time in Q&A and the workshop was soon over, but it taught me a valuable lesson: To write is to listen. As a writer, I sometimes think that to write is to talk, to relieve myself of my incessant need to communicate, but my writing is much better when I'm listening.

To pray is to listen. God wants me to bare my soul to him, but he also wants to bare his heart and thoughts to me. Maybe God doesn't just want to be talked to or talked at; he wants to have a conversation with us. He sent Jesus so we could converse with him personally, face to face.

We can have some really cool moments with God through other people and through all of our technology and machines, but the old-school method is tried and true. You, your Bible and your soul ready to be transparent. That's what knowing God boils down to. It's not the "cool" thing and it's not the "in" thing to post on your timeline, but it's spending time with the One who is the center of all life, the giver of all peace. The One who is love and hope. The only One who always keeps his promises, whose motives are never questionable, who thought us worthy enough to send his Son to give his life. That's no cliché. That is worth living and dying for, worth giving your time for.

My challenge to you is to take your busy, tired, scattered mind and quiet yourself before God. Close this chapter and sit. Maybe you'll learn to love when it rains. Maybe you'll love it so much that sometimes, when a storm brings lightning and thunder to your

window or anxious thoughts to your mind, you'll unplug everything and listen while God is doing his work. Then ultimately you
will let God do his work in you.

BREAKING RHYTHM

୬୰ Spend two minutes in silence. What does it teach you about
yourself?

୬୰ Ask someone close to you to talk for five minutes while you
listen. Jot down what you gather from what they say. What
did you learn about them? About yourself?

୬୰ Read Psalm 23 from the first person, as if you were listening
to God say it to you ("I am your Shepherd, you shall not
want"). Jot down what you gather. What did you learn about
God? What did you learn about yourself?

EIGHT

BEAT BOX

The first time I heard the phrase "think outside the box," I was probably sitting in a corporate boardroom "brainstorming." Here the term was used out of context because we weren't being asked to "think outside the box." We were being asked to think out of one box into a slightly larger one. *OH*

"Outside the box" has become cliché, so a lot of us don't believe it and don't live it either. In *Creative Habit*, Twyla Tharp writes that before we can "get out of the box," we have to start with the box.

The box is more than likely not a physical place. The box is how we limit ourselves, God and other people with our thoughts, perspectives and expectations. In essence, our box becomes the seat of our self-imposed limitations.

We typically build our box around three words: *predictable, comfortable* and *convenient. Predictable* because it gives us a false sense of control. *Comfortable* because we think we won't have to change. *Convenient* because we want everything to be easy. Anytime we find our life surrounded by those three words we are, brick by brick, building a box for ourselves.

GET UNPREDICTABLE

Sometimes God intends to let a story finish before the denouement with no resolution. Sometimes it seems like he ends his sonnet at the twelfth line and leaves me guessing his next move. Sometimes it feels like God doesn't tie up loose ends or wrap a pretty bow around anything, as if he prefers a question mark, comma or semi-colon instead of a period.

How do you typically respond when your routine is disrupted? When your plan isn't unfolding in the time you scheduled? When your ducks all crowd together, refusing to get in a row like distracted children? When your t's and i's scatter like ants from their disturbed hill and will not be crossed or dotted? I for one, think the world should stop until every ant, i, t and duck gets in its place. This rarely happens. For some disrespectful reason, the world goes on with no regard to my well-laid plans.

Breaking rhythm teaches me to hold to my routine and well-laid plans loosely. God is the ultimate planner. Scriptures and studies show that his ducks, ants, i's and t's are always in order. He's just got a darn good poker face, and no matter what tricks I try he will not reveal his hand. And oh, he plays it well.

Sometimes in the disruption of our routine, God finds a sweet spot to remind us he's the one in control. This is what it means for God to be sovereign: At any time, in any place, he can do whatever he wants to do, whenever and however he wants to do it. One thing you can trust: Whatever he does will work out for your good. How he manages to do that in every situation for everyone involved even when it makes no sense to our human pea brains, I don't understand. I suppose that is what makes him God.

This week practice unpredictability; create your own disruption. Take a different way home. Introduce yourself to someone you don't know. Move your toothbrush holder to the opposite side of the sink. Smile by only moving your nose. Do something different! Look for ways you can embrace interruption. Surrender your thoughts, worries, routine, ants, i's, t's and ducks to him, the sovereign God who's got it all mapped out and taken care of anyway.

The issue here is not throwing your routine out the window, but rather answering why you hold so tightly to it. There is always an issue when we hold too tightly to anything. Although this life is real and tangible, it is also temporary. It lives, breathes, dies and ceases to be. The irony and mastery of God is that all that is really real cannot be touched, is not tangible. The more we hold on to people and things and stake our existence, validation and worth on whether or not those people and things fail us, the less peaceful we are and the more we will find ourselves with hearts that turn away from God.

Sometimes the song changes; sometimes the dance is different. The goal of life is not to find one dance move and keep doing that for twenty years. The real goal is to keep dancing, never to let a change of song, scenery or step intimidate you back to the wall. God is a God of discipline and consistency, not a God of routine or religion. Jesus could have set up a system to flow and run for all his three years of ministry. It doesn't appear that Jesus was much about the system. It appears that he was about the heart of the matter, about the heart and about what matters, about knowing names, lives and stories, about loving and serving. This kind of system is hard to measure quantifiably.

Jesus never healed anyone the same way twice. His life was not overly predictable. Instead of quoting Scriptures in a rote way, Jesus not only lived out what he said but told stories that acted as metaphors he knew his followers would be able to grasp. Jesus also did the unexpected. He went into the temple and turned over tables, leaving the place in a ruckus when he saw it being used for financial gain instead of a house of worship. He kept company with misfits, rebels and outcasts, kicked it with tax collectors, going to their parties and social gatherings. He did all the things that many people expected a "messiah" would never do.

I come from a family of musicians and storytellers. Watching their lives has taught me that life is a lot more like a loop in a piece of music than a chronological line to be calculated. Try to bob your head to the loop of your life. Dig its melody and embrace the refrain until you can sing it wholeheartedly. Ask Jesus to teach you to be unpredictable just like he is.

Do Something Uncomfortable

A lot of days, God is more like my personal trainer, pulling the sheets off my warm body while the morning's cool invades every one of my pores. Except he doesn't bark or yell. He just says, "Let's go," and stands there until I squint out of bed, grumble about it being too early or say under my breath, "Don't you ever sleep?"

He says, "No, I don't sleep." I wince. *Kind of early for sarcasm*, I think but don't say. He knows I thought it anyway. He's got these workouts that build my character. As soon as I get comfortable, lean back with my hands behind my head or rest on my laurels, he switches the program and refuses to let my muscles get used to that same exercise. He constantly challenges me.

What was the last moment in life that challenged you? The danger in getting comfortable is that comfortable never pushed anybody to do anything revolutionary. No one ever leaned back on goose down pillows and said, "I better change the world." Being without, not having enough, feeling helpless and hopeless is what gives us courage, character and perseverance. James said it this way:

> Consider it pure joy, my brothers and sisters, whenever you
> face trials of many kinds, because you know that the testing

of your faith produces perseverance. Let perseverance finish its work so that you may be mature and complete, not lacking anything. (James 1:2-4)

The Bible says that Jesus didn't even have a place to lay his head (Matthew 8:20; Luke 9:58). Yes, this means Jesus didn't have an SUV, a condo, an iPod or the latest fashions. I'm not downing these things, and this is by no means a guilt trip for those of us who have them. But Jesus didn't have a comfortable life; that was God's calling for him. There may be many times God will ask us to forsake our comfort for his cross, to surrender to him in the face of denying ourselves.

Jesus went through the wilderness, went hungry and had no luxury, and sometimes not a lot of time to rest. Jesus will always be calling and leading us to surrender, and some of that surrendering will involve our comfort. He came to serve not to be served, to lift up the Father not himself. This is also our purpose and calling. Anytime you find yourself relishing your comfy life, it is time to question how closely you are following Jesus. We should wear our comfort loosely and be willing to give it up for Jesus' sake.

CHEATING AND CONVENIENCE

The easy way never worked for me. I remember the first and last time I cheated in school. I was in seventh-grade Honors English. My regular teacher had taken ill, and we students had been, in our eyes, blessed with a substitute—a nice, sweet substitute, which meant she was a prime candidate to be ignored and never minded. She adhered tightly to our teacher's lesson plan, giving us homework assignments like a real honors class. The nerve of her! One particular story from our textbook was hideously boring, and she wanted us to complete the questions at the end in paragraph form.

I decided not to read said boring story, which prevented me from completing said questions. Smart honors students that we were, we discovered amongst ourselves by second period that only three of our classmates had completed the assignment. Being giving people, they relinquished their hard work to the rest of us slackers, which circulated among us like delicious but dirty gossip.

From my more studious classmates, I gathered that the story's central character, Harry, was trying to make an important decision. That's about all that stuck with me as I attempted to decipher the still budding cursive of my classmate. Assignment done and all turned in, by that Thursday I was focusing on my evening plans. My mom had agreed I could go and watch *Martin* at my BFF Kim's house. One of my favorite sitcoms from junior high, *Martin* was serious television and was even better watched with friends. I had no idea that doom was waiting for me in my second-to-last class of the day.

Miss Nice Sweet Substitute began class as usual by waiting for all of us to settle into our seats. She opened class by reading a definition from the dictionary for *honor*, which she proceeded to tell us, is what she thought this *honors* class was about. I still didn't realize we were in trouble until she mentioned angrily that had each of us read the story ourselves we would know the central character's name was *Harry*—not *Mary*, not *Larry* and definitely not *Darius*. She went on to say that we must have assumed her stupid for thinking she wouldn't be able to tell whose homework was actually completed by the worn, torn, tattered, and folded three assignments she discovered in her stack along with our fraudulent ones.

And then the teacher said the thing that Jeanne Brown's daughter never wanted to hear: She was going to call our parents. Not only that, but she had made photocopies of all of our papers and wanted them returned with a signature from our parents.

This put a humongous wrench in my plans to watch *Martin*. My mom, ironically similar in disposition to Miss Nice Sweet Substitute, was a sweet-faced woman who had no qualms about demonstrating why she should be respected, why she was the adult and you were the child.

Now I had a decision to make. Would I

a. Be chancy, take the risk that Miss Nice Sweet Substitute would forget to call or take the risk that even if she did call I would have enjoyed my show by then and in happiness I could take whatever punishment my sweet-faced but gangsta mom doled out?

Or would I

b. Forego *Martin* and BFF Kim just this once and fess up, tell my mom everything and plead with the court for mercy?

I chose option *b*. I knew I would get in more trouble for not having told my mom before the teacher.

I knew my mother. A single mom, she worked night shift, so when I got home from school she was typically asleep. This meant I would have to wake her to tell her of my indiscretion. I prepared my tears and sad, sobbing speech all the way home on the bus. I woke her up and sorrowfully told her about Larry and Harry and Mary and Darius. I told her how disappointed I was in myself. I went so far as to punish myself, suggesting no TV and phone for the rest of the week. It was Thursday, but still, hadn't I suffered enough?

My mom grew quiet, her gaze never leaving my face. I began to fear for my life. Her silence couldn't mean anything good. But my mom, who had no problems with disciplining in a physical manner, having been raised on North Carolina switches herself, instead went for the jugular, cutting off my communication with the outside world.

"You're right. You won't be watching TV or talking on the phone for the rest of the week. In fact, you won't be watching TV or talking on the phone for *six* weeks until I see that all your grades have come up to at least *B*s in all your classes. You will get five minutes of phone time every day to tell your friends that you can't talk on the phone. Now go in your room and finish your homework!"

Blast! Curses! She took my punishment and raised me six weeks! TV I could take. But no phone?! Then she had the nerve to make me be the bad guy: I would have to tell my friends that I couldn't discuss who liked whom, who had a crush on whom, who fought with whom, who wore what name brand, who saw which music video. All because I decided to write about Larry, Harry, Mary and Darius? I wanted Mom to tell my friends for me, give them the mean voice when they called. Then the next day I could blame her—flick my head back and say, "You know how moms do." My friends—they would have understood this. They would have filed her in the category we put all of our parents in—uncool and out of touch and always ruining some fun. But this time *I* was uncool. *I* would be out of touch. *I* had ruined my own fun. The nerve. Of. Me.

I share this story to tell you two things. One, don't cheat. Just don't. I mean, if you do, get the central character's name right, skim the story, get some clues for yourself.

Ahem. Sorry, I think I just ruined my own PSA. Back to the first part: Don't cheat. Read. Do your own homework. And for goodness' sake don't pass 'it around to a bunch of slackers. Save yourself. Practice homework abstinence. Don't give your homework away to every slick-talking classmate. You wouldn't want your name to end up getting passed around and copied, or wind up waiting for a parent's signature, now would ya? Because believe those well-meaning homework doers went down in our sinking ship along with us.

My other point: there is no easy way to get anything that's worth getting. If you've been skating by on easy street, you may just be near a serious bump in the road with no warning sign. Easy street only exists on movie sets. It's only a block long, the food isn't real, and once the shoot is over the fake citizens no longer say hello or speak to you. This life does not promise that everything you need will be within reach, like all the appliances in a New York apartment. You're going to work, you're going to sweat, you might even bleed, but you're going to have to give your all to something.

In Matthew 13:44, Jesus tells a story about the kingdom of heaven:

> The kingdom of heaven is like treasure hidden in a field. When a man found it, he hid it again, and then in his joy went and sold all he had and bought that field.

What is the "treasure" you would sell everything for? I hope that treasure is not public opinion, reputation or having your way all the time. There are several times in the New Testament where you find Jesus on his way to do something else but instead someone in need interrupts him. I don't respond well when someone else's needs or wants interfere with what I've planned for my schedule. Jesus lived a life of continual interruptions, with crowds edging in on his alone time and people stopping him to heal them or their workers or family members before he could take another step.

Want to follow Jesus? Prepare to be inconvenienced. Prepare for your life to no longer be about you. I am not advocating not taking care of yourself. You have to rest, eat and do the basic things you have to do in order to have anything to give to anyone else. I am advocating that we hold a lot less tightly to the idea of our lives being easy and convenient. There are crowds of hurting souls who need the light you have, and they may find you when you are getting ready to head home, leave work or go out to the store. Like Jesus, may our hearts break for them and love them enough to offer the power of this miraculous God we serve and love.

The boxes we build for ourselves are not necessarily bad in and of themselves, but wanting our lives to be safe, convenient, comfortable and predictable is the antithesis of following Jesus. If we are really going to follow him and his rhythm we are going to give up our boxes. We're going to slide all of our chips to the middle and gamble everything on God. He's the only gamble worth our everything.

On Making Yourself Small

A lot of my life-changing moments seem to happen in coffee houses. Maybe because coffee houses are in-between places, and my friends and I are all doing what we can to skate by while we attempt to build the lives we think we want. Coffee spots create a nice place to conveniently meet up between the end of the workday and dinner without paying for dinner. This doesn't really matter, though. With the right girlfriend I have talked the coffee house until closing. There's something about that small table and having to lean in and listen. I always leave contemplative, challenged. Sometimes I leave praying—praying about my own selfish attitude or praying for the woman across from me to know God's grace or praying that I would stop settling for second or third best.

One particular afternoon I was sitting across from my coifed, polished, professional good friend. She was finally dating a man she loved, except she wasn't sure if it would last, wasn't sure if they had a future together. He was a freewheeling entrepreneur, and she was climbing the corporate ladder. Their differences drew them together. They both wanted to feel completely, comfortably safe with someone.

My friend had a vision for her life: to pursue her career and eventually get married. The man she was involved with didn't seem to have the same priorities. Basically, she was frustrated to the point of wanting to choke him, to leave the imprint of her fingers on his neck till he knew that she wanted their relationship to be more, that she needed his commitment. But she didn't choke him—first, because she's not a violent person, and second, because she didn't want to scare him away.

I sipped my latte to keep from putting my foot in my mouth. I put my latte back on the table and sighed.

"I worry that you're making yourself small," I said.

"What do you mean?" she said.

"I mean, it seems like you're only being the part of yourself that enables you to keep this relationship, which is really no relationship at all because you're not being your full self."

She thought for a while, and we both took sips of our lattes.

"I've been doing that for so long I don't know how to start being my full self," she said.

"Maybe you start with being honest a moment at a time. If you love this guy and he loves you, you should be able to be honest with each other, right?"

She nodded, and soon after we grabbed our purses to go because we had talked ourselves until it got dark outside. On my way home, I turned my radio down and thought about the whole idea of making ourselves small. It's funny how it's easy to say something to someone else until you have to live it too.

I'm not in any way going against the idea of being humble. I'm talking about the instances when you pretend that certain things are okay with you when they're not, when you choose not to be the unique person God created you to be because you worry what other people will think of you. We've all had moments when we folded ourselves up to fit into some box. The irony is that we assume and get angry that we're selling ourselves short trying to fit into someone else's box when the truth is we are limiting ourselves to fit into our own narrow idea of who we are, what we can be and who God created us to be.

THE RIGHT WAY TO CONFORM

More than likely any box you've built for yourself is based on fear. As scary as it is, you have to face every one of those fears or you will continue to settle for less than you should. When we hear a commonly used phrase like "Get out of the box," we sometimes assume that means we need to be someone different. The only way to really get outside the box—the only way to really be unique or original—is to be yourself.

God is original, and he made each of us unique. We end up settling for the boxes we build when we are comparing ourselves to other people and trying so hard to be like other people.

Please don't let this book or any of these statements fool you. By my nature I'm a conformist. Most of my life I've done a pretty good job at following the crowd around me. Some call this being a peacemaker; some call it being a people pleaser. Whatever it's called, it's usually about making sure I don't ruffle any feathers.

There's only one time the Bible talks about conforming: "Do not conform to the pattern of this world, but be transformed by the renewing of your mind" (Romans 12:2). Maybe this Scripture means we should quit conforming and become transformists instead. Sometimes we get caught in being nice and placid more than we focus on really being ourselves, exactly as God made us. I used to think to be a believer in community meant going along with what everyone else says—with no questions asked, not many opinions given and plenty of agreeing all the time. But when we are not ourselves we are not being who God created us to be; we are being who we think we need to be for people to like us or accept us. When we do that, who are people actually liking or accepting? Some character we have crafted to keep ourselves from being hurt or abandoned or rejected.

Jesus definitely experienced being hurt, abandoned and rejected. We should expect nothing less for ourselves; if there's any pattern we're supposed to be conformed to, it's Jesus'. And that's ironic because his pattern was so unlike a pattern—it was organic and not bullet-pointed, not formulaic, not an easily calculated equation.

I sometimes still feel like a new kid, holding a notebook with my life's question on it, hoping someone will please answer it and tell me I'm okay and I'm worth it and I'm not crazy. It's nice to have people who love me look at that question on my notebook, scrawled out in Sharpie, and say, "I love you. You're okay. You're worth it to me." But some days the people we love aren't available and we only get their voicemail, they don't respond immediately to our email, or they miss the subtext in the way we are trying to get our question answered. So they small talk about their day while we are left insecure and nearly in tears trying to hear something good about ourselves.

Yeah, I have those days. Everyone does—even people you'd imagine would never have such moments. Even though these other people love us, we've reached the end of what they can do for us and the beginning of what only God can be to us. We need him. He's the only one with the answer to our life's question. He is the only answer to life's question. He's the reason we're never alone.

Even though I have called myself a Christian for many years, I am still searching for God—not because God is playing some mean game of hide and seek with me, but because it takes me time to sift through my muck and mud and sin and distraction to get down to the fact that I need him and he loves me. He's not some exacting father who doles out his love based on whether or not I perform well. God is not a stage parent, waiting with hugs when you get all your steps right and coldly driving you home when you forget your lines. God is a father, a loving parent who doesn't have the limits of human patience. He has patience and love that never end.

I just wish, for myself and for all of us, that we'd see him as he really is. I wish we could all stop making him out to be so mean, so human, stop making him match our imperfections, stop looking for anything or anyone else to fill us up in his place. As humans we're always trying to be satisfied. This is why we smoke, eat, have sex and seek people's approval. It's part of the reason we text, tweet and Facebook. We want to be satisfied. We want to be validated. But nothing and no one satisfies like God. All other satisfaction is momentary and temporary. And the only way we can be satisfied by God and with God is to dance with him the same way the disciples walked with Jesus. Every day. Sweaty. Smelly. Tired. With questions. With doubts.

Walking with God didn't become impossible when Jesus physically left the earth. Jesus came so we can truly walk with God with no middleman or mediator. This is why Jesus told his disciples that "the Advocate, the Holy Spirit, whom the Father will send in my name, will teach you all things and will remind you of everything I have said to you" (John 14:26).

I didn't always understand the Holy Spirit. He is God, so my human brain will never completely understand him. I've thought at times he was spooky, scary, but I'm learning that the Holy Spirit is not a Christian version of Casper the Friendly Ghost. He is not cartoony. He is holy. He is our teacher. He is the One who helps us walk in Jesus' footsteps. Walking with God, being in step with the Holy Spirit, means living life with God every day—not just when you're at church, not just when you're around other believers. Walking with God involves cultivating in your soul the realization that God is truly there, with you, right now while you're reading this—and when you're in your car, at home, at your job or in conversation. God is there, knowing and keeping record of every tear you cry, every time you laugh, every breath, every note, every passing thought.

I used to think following God, having a relationship with him, was based on occasional moments. I felt I was meeting God sometimes during a really good concert, when I was experiencing all those feelings of worship and connection. Then I wouldn't really think about them until the next good concert I went to. I've realized that following God is not just about being momentous, but it is literally moment by moment choosing to trust and love and hang on and hang in there—when you feel good and when you don't, when it all makes sense and when it doesn't. Life with Christ doesn't happen just when I lift my hands. It's steady like a heartbeat, like a rhythm, and you learn to follow it, learn to know its pace, its rise and fall. I want to follow God like that.

Maybe the truth is that Jesus is the transformist, using truth to make us all into who we were created to be. If we're going to conform to anything, let's conform to him. Let's blend in with what he says and does. God isn't just trying to transform us into better versions of ourselves; he's transforming us to look more and more like him. That's the kind of conformist we should all want to be.

BREAKING RHYTHM

- Describe an area in your life where you feel too comfortable. What is one thing you can do to stretch out of your comfort zone?

- How can you practice unpredictability this week?

- Reflect on Romans 12:2. How can you renew your mind this week?

NINE

BAGGAGE CHECK

my mother's mother
gave her her first set of luggage
blue with a hard rough exterior
two thumbs on latch
opened with a metal click clack
here
my mother learned what to pack
how to go
when to leave

mother bird
left to build a nest to provide for her young
plus fend for herself
so she raised me to fly
except I inherited her luggage

AMENA BROWN, *BAGS*

*M*ost women are obsessed with bags. Some women carry big bags, filled with their whole life plus a bunch of items from Walgreens. Some women carry tiny bags with barely enough room to fit lip gloss and a cell phone. My obsession with bags started when I was about six. It was the first Easter that I have clear memories of. My grandma believed Easter wasn't Easter unless you got a new dress, new shoes, stockings and a pocketbook to match. Yes, *pocketbook*. In small-town North Carolina there's no such thing as a purse. All of the women carry pocketbooks.

That year my grandma got me a nice, pastel Easter dress with tulle underneath so the skirt billowed out when I sat on the church pew. She wore a nice fitted suit with knee-length skirt and patent leather shoes, which of course meant she had to have a pillbox hat and patent leather pocketbook to match. Previous Easters I had envied my grandma's pocketbook with its shine and the little pucker sound it made every time she opened and closed its snap clutch, plus the Starlight mints and Werther's Originals she always seemed to hide in there. When I was six years old, my grandma gave me my own pocketbook. I was free to stuff it with tissue, crayons, mints and doodads.

Life is a trip, which means we've all got bags. I learned about pocketbooks from my grandma, learned how to pack luggage military-style from my mom. That's the thing about bags. It's not just that we carry them; it's how we learn to pack them and what it means to us to have those bags.

Maybe you've heard the metaphor Erykah Badu laid out in her song "Bag Lady," about all of the bags we carry from our past that keep us from love, from our full potential, from our destinies. I did what any good poet would do: I wrote a poem about it, or at least I tried to, but it was hard to finish. Sometimes when a poem, story or article is digging into your issues it does that—gets way harder to finish than you'd expected.

BAGGAGE CLAIM

I took my first airplane trip when I was four years old. My parents were separated, my mom and I living in North Carolina and my dad stationed in California. My mom packed my bag to visit my dad for a summer, including all the pertinent clothes and favorite toys and books. My parents would divorce a couple of years later, so this was the first of many plane trips, as I shuttled back and forth between their two homes.

I grew up with parents who at various times in my childhood were in two different branches of the military. If there was anything I learned how to do, it was pack a bag. I learned to make new friends quickly, which meant I also learned the pain of losing them too soon. By the time I was nine, I was flying by myself with flight attendants as my chaperones.

Some people learn to hoard bags, packing up the things that are given to them and keeping them, no matter how worthless or weighty. They have to learn to let things go, to get rid of the bags that so easily beset them. I learned early on how to live like a vagabond. I had to learn how to unpack my bags and find home.

OVERWEIGHT

Traveling in airplanes most of my life has taught me a lot about baggage. I have experienced many moments to the tune of Pullman wheels squeaking against linoleum, the rhythm of quickly closed zipper compartments, the sound of canvas and leather scooting past each other. The security advisory in the airport is all about the items and bags we carry, how closely we attend to them and, above all, how much they weigh.

When I completed my first CD project I was traveling to the first speaking engagement where I would be selling them. When you've never completed a CD project you overestimate how many you'll need; you clearly assume you are this generation's one-person version of the Beatles and that your CD will go flying off the merchandise table before you can make change for a hundred. So I stuffed my luggage with five hundred CDs and arrived at the ticket counter with a smile. The ticket agent smiled back, asked for my boarding pass and license and then asked for me to place the bags I was checking on the scale. Even though my bicep almost snapped when I lifted the bag, I kept the smile going.

"Ma'am, your bag is overweight."

Overweight is a word no woman wants to hear. It doesn't matter if we're talking about my luggage, my hips or a sack of flour, *overweight* is never a positive. The ticket agent told me how much it would cost me to check the bag, which for a recent college grad like me was over budget ("budget" being *free*). I unzipped my luggage, airing my unmentionables, to even out the weight by putting half the CDs in my clothes bag, squishing them between jeans and toiletries.

It was more worth it to me to keep my stuff than to chance leaving it, even if it meant delaying my trip. This is the problem with bags from our past. They keep us from reaching our destination in life. When we continue to carry them, not only do they weigh us down, they cost us. Sometimes we need a ticket agent in life, to ask us if we've left our bags unattended, if we are carrying bags for anyone else, to help us choose which bags we will check and which bags we will carry on.

BAGS UNATTENDED

We don't carry the bags of our past in our arms like physical luggage; we carry them in our hearts. This means how we love, how we allow ourselves to be loved, whether we reach or never tap into our fullest potential—all these are connected to what our hearts carry. That's why Proverbs 4:23 says, "Above all else, guard your heart, for everything you do flows from it."

Leaving unforgiveness unattended leads to bitterness. Leaving hurt unattended can lead to depression. Leaving insecurity unattended leads to pride. Leaving anger unattended leads to rage. This unattended baggage causes us to hurt people, to push people who love us away, to distance ourselves from the truth and from God.

Guarding our hearts means protecting the center of our being, which we always carry with us. Attending to our bags means examining what we've been carrying.

I have an obsession with the TV show *Hoarders*. I have sat in front of the TV unable to tear myself away from each story chronicling the process of helping someone with a compulsive hoarding disorder. The disorder involves keeping trash and shopping excessively, and it leads to corroded collectibles blocking hallways, doorjambs and windows. These things keep the hoarder from getting out, but they also keep anyone from getting in.

It's easy to scoff at a compulsive hoarder, thinking all the hoarder needs to do is clean up their house and throw things away. But if someone had to peer into the house of our hearts, that clean-up job might not seem so simple. A hoarder keeps things around under the illusion that someday they will use them, someday they will give it to someone, someday they will have more room for the items—but someday never comes.

Many of us do the same thing. We hold onto grudges, hoping to wield them at the person who offended us, hiding our insecurities behind selfish pride to keep a false sense of feeling good about ourselves. If it were as simple as cleaning up and throwing things away we would have done that already.

Hoarders have to process why they can't get rid of things, dig to the source of what they think they are protecting themselves from by building a shell of stuff to surround them. In turn, we have to process why we can't let things go. What do we fear our lives will be like if we forgive, admit our weakness and release our anger? When we excavate to discover the root of what we have left unattended in our hearts, we can dig it up from the source, clean up and throw things away.

Carrying Bags for Someone Else

When I would fly to visit my dad, my mom would let me use her luggage, which she inherited from her mom. This also happens in life. Sometimes you've been carrying baggage so long you can't recall how you wound up with it in the first place. Examining your bags is about ownership, taking responsibility for the decisions you've made but also discarding things you are carrying for anyone else.

Before my husband and I were even dating I knew I wanted to marry him. It wasn't just because of the warm fuzzies I felt every time he walked into a room, but mostly because he met all of the character requirements I'd written in my journal years before we knew each other, things only God knew I prayed about. I wanted my future husband to be smart and fun to be around. I wanted him to be my friend, to be honest, to follow Jesus for himself, to be someone who knew his calling in life and was pursuing that.

It's amazing how one conversation can change everything. Matt and I were friends, purely platonic, never-flirted-with-each-other friends. He DJed at my open mic. We recorded together in the studio. Our friendship developed over rhymes and beats and lyrics. One night we went to see a hip hop artist perform and we grabbed dinner afterward. We talked about art, how our journey as believers informed our art, what it meant to be an artist and a Christian, how we both hoped our art would shine God's light whether we were in a sanctuary or a smoky, hole-in-the-wall club.

We talked about how we both were getting teased about how much time we spent together. We talked about dating and whether we each had hope that God had somebody for us. We'd shared our past heartbreaks. I told him about my break-ups, and he told me about the painful demise of his first marriage. We drove away from each other that night talking to each other by phone on our way home.

"So, I know why I'm single. But why are you single?" he asked.

"Because I don't put out," I said.

We both laughed, but then he said, "No, seriously. Guys wouldn't date you because of that?"

"Yep. It's happened more than once," I said.

"That's crazy. The fact that you made that decision and stuck to it is really attractive."

He already had a lot of cool points with me, but that comment in particular really upped his cool points bank account.

"Some guys don't want to date me because I want to be about Jesus, and they don't want to be about that. Some of them don't dig what I do for a living," I said.

"Okay, well describe him. The type of guy you want to be with, what's he like?" he asked.

"He lives for Jesus but could handle being in a room where they spin Jay-Z. He knows something of his purpose in life and is pursuing that. He's fun and my friend, and I can talk to him," I said.

At this point, I'm feeling pretty silly because I'm basically describing him in detail. So I go on. "Look, I've got something I need to say. It might be awkward, but I think our friendship can take it."

"Let me help you out," he interrupted. "I think you're incredible. I find you attractive on several levels. You asked me if I have hope that God has someone for me, and I have hope because of you."

This was not at all how I thought the conversation would go. I didn't know he felt the same way about me that I had been feeling about him at all those open mics and studio sessions. I decided to ask for some clarity.

"So, you're saying you want to date just me, like exclusively?"

Considering my dating past, this question was merited. I had learned my lesson in not clarifying, by dating the guy who totally wanted to hang out with me as long as I was cool with him dating three other women too.

"Yeah, I want to date you exclusively. That's what I mean," he said.

In a couple of hours of conversation our platonic friendship became a dating relationship. We grew into love without the typical pretenses. He'd already seen me in my sweat pants, T-shirt and flip-flops. Our first date was sweet and awkward, neither one of us quite knowing how to dress up and look cute to hang out with each other. We sat next to each other on the same side of the booth in a little Chinese restaurant, so nervous and excited we hardly touched our food. Two weeks into our relationship, we knew we wanted to get married—a realization that was exhilarating and frightening.

I was excited to be in love, but nervous that maybe I didn't know how to be in a good relationship, fearful that a good thing might be too good to be true. As Matt and I dated and spent time together, his actions and how he kept his word to me showed me even more why I had so much respect for him as a friend.

After he proposed and we were planning our wedding, I found myself obsessed with reading and learning as much as I could about having a healthy marriage. I'd ask anyone I knew who was married for advice on how to stay together. I wanted to know the pitfalls so we didn't have to experience them. My fear of failing at marriage was driving me to want to control our relationship more than trust the One who'd brought us together.

During our premarital counseling I realized I was putting all of this pressure on myself to make our relationship and future marriage work because it didn't work for my parents. Somewhere inside I'd decided if I made a relationship work that it would make up for my parents' divorce and save me from having one too.

I also realized this was why I had stayed in bad relationships in the past. I wanted so bad to finish and not abandon a relationship in what felt like *in medias res*—not at the beginning or the end, but in the middle. Those relationships weren't about whether the person and I were a good match for each other. They were me hoping to make it up to my six-year-old self and my thirty-year-old self at the same time. I was carrying baggage that wasn't my bag to carry.

I had been carrying this burden about wanting to have a good relationship because my parents divorced and I didn't want that to happen to me. Their experience made me fear that something was wrong with me, that I didn't have the goods to maintain a healthy relationship.

One night after a premarital counseling session I confessed this burden to Matt. I told him how I desperately wanted our marriage to work because I felt it was up to me to make a marriage work for us and for my parents. But I told him I realized it wasn't my responsibility to have a good marriage to redeem my parents' divorce. That was something God did and had done in their lives. In my marriage to Matt I had to be willing to put in the work required. Having a good marriage wasn't something I could do by myself or that Matt and I could do by ourselves. We needed God. This was a bag I had to surrender to my Father who is love and teaches us love, the One who could help us to have a great marriage.

Sometimes we carry bags as reminders of what we don't want in life. These bags house our fears, and you will never live your life the way God intended when you live based on your fears. Relinquish any bags that aren't your own to the One whose shoulders are more than big enough to carry them.

SUBJECT TO SEARCH

If I were ever to imagine myself an animal, I would be a bird. Not a bird in a zoo or stuck in a cage. I would want to fly in my natural habitat. To me, flying meant having the freedom to be exactly who I was meant to be, no more and no less.

God used my parents' divorce to give me a life of flying. This helped me to realize that life is a lot like flying on planes. We all have a seat and a destination. We all get to carry a certain number of bags. If we carry more bags than we're allotted, if we carry bags that weigh more than we're allotted, we pay a hefty price. At a ticket counter, you pay baggage fees, but in life you pay through loss of relationships, lack of peace and forgiveness, frustration and complacency.

Not all bags are bad. We need to carry certain things with us for the journey, but some of the bags we carry are preventing us from flying. This means it's time for some baggage check, and I don't mean handing your bags to TSA personnel. It's time to assess your bags, which ones to keep and which to let go of.

Our baggage check is not at the ticket counter; it's at the cross, where we can surrender our bags to Jesus, who already carried everything we're dealing with. When the Bible says, "By His stripes we are healed" (Isaiah 53:5 NKJV), it means Jesus carried all of the things wrong with us, that through his sacrifice we are made whole. Jesus has already carried all the things that are weighing us down.

TIME TO UNPACK

Once I realized Jesus had carried the weight of my baggage, I knew I still wasn't done with bags. For me, bags and luggage were symbols of leaving and being left, of being ready at a moment's notice to pack up and move on with no thought of who or what I was leaving behind. Others had left me in this way—family members and friends who seemed to easily pack up who they were and leave town with minimal goodbye and no apparent sign of missing me. I also had left people I cared about, the threads of connection wearing thin as the distance between us stretched wider.

While I have been trying to write about bags I realized there is a message in there for me. Even though I've grown up and made a life of traveling, it's time for me to forsake my emotional vagabond ways and unzip my bag, unpack, put my clothes in a dresser or on hangers and put everything in its place. I may have been left, but I have done enough leaving. It is time for me to find a safe place to stay.

God is still teaching me what the Scriptures say about being safe in the shadow of his wing, that just the mention of his name is my refuge. With Jesus, I'm safe to unpack all the things I've been holding on to: the people I need to forgive, the hurt I need to let go of, the anger I need to dig underneath, the insecurities I attempt to disguise. This unpacking is necessary because as long as I'm jet-setting to the next place on the itinerary I'm not taking the time to examine what I'm dragging along with me.

I always envied my friends who grew up in the same house with two parents their whole life, whose families still have the same phone number they had when we were kids. I never knew that life. Underneath so many of the wrong things I've done was this quest to be at home somewhere with someone, when the whole time God was trying to show me that my safest home is with him. In him are love and peace and finding who I am and why I am.

So I've learned how to pack pretty well, but I'm also learning how to unpack my luggage and sift through what I find there. I'm learning to let God and others love me despite the stuff I carry. I'm also learning to let go of the bags that weigh me down, to leave more space in my life for things I should keep.

Whatever bags you bring with you, it's never too late to surrender them. It's never too late to stop running and leaving when things get tough or too close for comfort. You're not reading this by accident. Start now: Unpack one of your bags. Get rid of the things you were never meant to carry, keep what's important and learn how to be at home with God and in your own skin.

BREAKING RHYTHM

⁓ Describe what your emotional baggage would look like if it were physical luggage.

⁓ Choose one thing in your heart or your home to let go of. Write down what it is and why you are letting it go. Share those details with someone.

TEN

FINDING THE BREAK BEAT

*C*heck the scene: Rows of long cafeteria tables. Smells like Teen Spirit and Cool Water. Two boys with baseball caps turned to the back, alternating the rhythm of fists and flat hands on the table, mixed in with beat boxing. British Knights, Reeboks, Air Jordans and K-Swiss tennis shoes tapping the beat under the table. A crowd is forming, a circle developing: the cipher. Many times this was the scene in my high school cafeteria. Everybody would nod their heads to the beat until someone leaned into the circle and attempted to emcee by freestyling.

The term *emcee* is technically an abbreviation for "master or mistress of ceremonies," but the heart of being an emcee is also to move the crowd. What gave the emcee the edge above a poet or songwriter was the ability to freestyle: to take what you see, where you are, and create something new on the spot. Freestyling is the hip hop version of improvisation. Improvisation is what made genres of music like jazz famous. Freestyling meant being able to construct rhymes or bits of music in your head, a line at a time, without really knowing what will come next until you get there.

When I fell in love with hip hop as a teenager, my friends Aron,

Tawfiq and Chris became my tutors, passing me as many cassettes featuring female emcees as they could get their hands on. The poetry I'd come to love also lived in these rap lyrics. I listened to all the female emcees I could: Missy Eliot, Boss, Rage, Bahamadia, Lauryn Hill, Left Eye, Nonchalant, Monie Love, MC Lyte and Queen Latifah.

My friends tried to explain how to freestyle, but I did so much better if I had paper in front of me and time to write it down. I am a perfectionist, an oldest kid who grew up slightly shy and mostly nerdy. Making things up on the fly never suited me. Thus my rap career was short lived. Truth is, I settled on becoming a poet because with poetry I could write rhymes to my heart's content with no regard to freestyling or how many bars the verse was.

Today many people throw around the term *rapper*. This is a term I rarely use because I grew up with so much love for emcees. Sometimes rappers are people who, over a beat, can throw together some words that rhyme. Being an emcee involves craft, good writing and a knack for storytelling.

When I first read John 1, I imagined John was an emcee.

In the beginning was the Word, and the Word was with God, and the Word was God. He was with God in the beginning. (John 1:1-2)

Rocking an oversized hoodie and baggy jeans, John stands at a lone microphone on a small stage in a smoky room. Jesus has died, been resurrected and ascended, and the only way John can think to describe what he's seen is by writing words that flow like poetry.

Through him all things were made; without him nothing was made that has been made. In him was life, and that life was the light of all mankind. (John 1:3-4)

John remembers his crew, how they all left what was comfortable to follow this rabbi who promised eternal life, living water and never to leave them.

> The light shines in the darkness, and the darkness has not overcome it. . . . The true light that gives light to everyone was coming into the world. He was in the world, and though the world was made through him, the world did not recognize him. He came to that which was his own, but his own did not receive him. (John 1:5, 9-11)

John remembers how they scattered when Jesus was arrested—how one betrayed him, one denied him, one doubted him, but they all had forsaken him when he needed them most.

> Yet to all who did receive him, to those who believed in his name, he gave the right to become children of God—children born not of natural descent, nor of human decision or a husband's will, but born of God. (John 1:12-13)

John writes his words in rhythm, the same rhythm Jesus used to multiply the fishes and loaves, to cry out for another way in the garden of Gethsemane, to ask forgiveness for those who had no idea they needed forgiving.

> The Word became flesh and made his dwelling among us. We have seen his glory, the glory of the one and only Son, who came from the Father, full of grace and truth. (John 1:14)

I imagine John looking into the crowd and seeing those disciples who had walked with Jesus and those who had begun to walk the Way from the stories of those who'd seen him. I picture him freestyling with a renegade crew, maybe a crew you'd be scared to walk down the street beside, a crew you wouldn't respect at first glance because they didn't seem like the kind of people the Son of God should cavort with. But he loved them.

Jesus taught them his beat, taught them to freestyle with what they had. He followed a different groove that only the Spirit can give. Told them stories in a language they could understand, to a beat they could live to. He demonstrated why he is the author and finisher of our faith.

Maybe Jesus is an emcee too, the true Master of Ceremonies, freestyling and rhyming parables, speaking life into our lives while spinning stories of truth, holiness and righteousness. I want to learn to rock to his rhythm. To hear his music, sit at his feet and listen to his stories. Maybe he wants to teach me to improvise with what I've got and what he gives me and watch him make beautiful music out of it.

PERMISSION TO MOVE FREELY

Moving to Jesus' rhythm calls for you to release your inhibitions. It means you start caring a whole lot less about what people think and a whole lot more about making the best of the moment you have right in front of you.

There's room for freestyling, for feeling the beat in your bones and letting it move you, for rocking the boogie to the beat of an internal drum. There's freedom for the kind of dance you do when you have on ugly pajamas, your favorite song and a house full of no one to be embarrassed in front of.

This is the dance you have to free yourself to do because it teaches you to care more about being present, about having fun and living this moment to the utmost, than about keeping up with unrealistic expectations or with people who are honestly always going to be richer or prettier or more well-mannered than you. Who wants to constantly go after a bar so deceptively high that you can never reach it? Freeing yourself means no more worries about things not being how you expected they would be.

Rules of Improv

I took an acting class once, not because I hoped to become the next Julia Roberts but because I do stage work and wanted to expand my repertoire. The class met on a weekly basis and rotated the types of things we worked on each week between cold reads, partner scenes, improvisations and screen work. The improvisation week was my most nervous.

Improv, like creativity, has its rules. The genius of improvisation is not that you can do whatever you want, however you want, it's that you take the structure of an art and tinker with it until you come up with something fresh and new. Creativity works the same way. I used to think creativity was this flighty experience where structure, establishment or the man couldn't hold you down, where you could freewheel your ideas anytime, anyplace. But now I know that creativity is at its best when operating within the structure of discipline. Creativity, like improvisation, doesn't need to run wild; it just needs a place to play.

In acting improv, the stage is your place to play. Our acting teacher would call us to the stage two at a time, sometimes telling us the scene and what characters we were to play or sometimes letting our classmates pick for us. Sometimes your scene was in the oddest place with the weirdest person: in outer space with an alien's mother, in an office with your boss who is a seven-year-old girl, in a boxing ring with your science teacher. No matter what the situation, you had to go with it until the teacher stopped you.

Sometimes our teacher would tell us the scene—let's say, a classroom—and make us start the scene without knowing what our characters were. It would be up to one of us on stage to decide. My partner might decide to be a talking chalkboard at which point I want to say, "Chalkboards don't talk. What kind of conversation am I supposed to have with you?" Learning the rules of improv taught me some things about life and about God.

ACCEPT YOUR SCENE

Start with a yes and see where that takes you.

TINA FEY, *BOSSYPANTS*

———— ⊶⊷ ————

The old Carl didn't think he was enough for anybody. I thought
if I said yes to things, and got involved with people, then
sooner or later they'd find out I'm not enough. I didn't
think I had anything to share. But now I know that
what I have to share is pretty huge, and I
want to share it with you.

CARL ALLEN (JIM CARREY), IN *YES MAN*

———— ⊶⊷ ————

It always baffled me how Jesus showed up on the scene, looked at the disciples fishing and collecting taxes, announced, "Come follow me," and they dropped their nets, numbers and lives to go with him. I used to think either Jesus had a really authoritative voice or the disciples saw something in him that meant he was offering a better life than the life they knew.

It seems the disciples were familiar with the "yes, and" rule of improv. No matter what my improv partner said I had to accept and go with it. I couldn't question or debunk because that would take time away from the task at hand, seeing the scene through until the end. I may have had my own ideas about how my partner and I could have been husband and wife or son and mother, but if my partner decides to be a fairy, I have to go with it and improvise a way to make that work. Yes, and . . .

Imagine if the disciples had said to Jesus, "Uh, whoa, let's back up a minute, Rabbi. So where exactly am I following you to? What kind of budget do you have for this? What is my role here? What's my motivation?"

The disciples didn't ask Jesus a thing at the moment. They went on to follow him, when they understood, when they were confused, when they had questions, when they had it all wrong. They said, "Yes, and." This requires surrender and complete trust in the One who leads us.

When God asks me to love someone who is difficult to love, to forgive someone or myself, to give of my time or resources when I want to be selfish, I want my answer to be "Yes, and" instead of "But, um."

"Yes, and" means I have to accept my scene, my current place in life. Beyond accepting, I jump in and do the best I can with it. If my improv partner wants to be a fairy, then maybe I can be Tinker Bell. I have to respect what my partner creates. I also must accept what my Father creates, knowing whatever scene he builds for me is for my good.

DOING THE WORK

There are no mistakes, only opportunities.

TINA FEY, *BOSSYPANTS*

———— ⌾⌾⌾ ————

Performing poetry, I've learned a rhythm of writing, drafting, performing the piece in front of an audience and then going back in secret to perfect the piece. My acting class did not afford me such luxury.

My acting teacher was no Paula Abdul, who made contestants feel so good on early seasons of *American Idol*. He was more Simon Cowell, a blunt professor who was not going to shield us from critique and criticism. One day we were working on two-person im-

provisation scenes. The scene was a living room. The two characters were a couple. One of them had been cheating; the other had
just found out. I played the wife who had been cheating. I was already in the scene. My now angry husband was entering the scene.

He did what most beginning actors would do: stormed into the
scene, slamming the door behind him because that's what angry
people do. I tried to summon up some tears but I couldn't find
them so I settled on an ugly, crying face.

My teacher stopped us before he could throw up in his mouth a
little bit. He turned to my stage husband and said, "What were you
doing before you came into this scene?"

"Standing behind the door."

"Exactly the problem. I don't mean what *you* were doing. I mean,
what were you doing in character. What was your *character* doing?"

My stage husband thought for a minute.

"Always know the moment before. Don't lean on what you think
angry or sad or excited looks like. Think about the moment before
until you really get angry," our teacher said. "According to the
Meisner method, acting is not faking it or telling a lie; acting is
being truthful. So you can't just pound your fist because that's
what you think people do when they get angry. You have to de-
velop enough story for your character so that you *can* get angry."

So my stage husband started creating back story, about how
he found out I was cheating from a mutual friend, how he
couldn't believe it, how he was seething all the way home in
rush-hour traffic.

My acting teacher nodded. "Now we're getting someplace.
Okay, let's switch the scene. Still a living room. Still a married
couple. This time you're walking in from a good day, and she's
upset with you. Do not walk into this scene until you know the
moment before."

So my stage husband walked out and I busied myself fake-cleaning our fake living room until he finally entered looking happy, as if he just got paid a bonus. I'm trying my best to look pissed off, annoyed, but I hadn't yet figured out what I was ticked off about. I started rattling off random reasons, and my actor teacher said, "Scene!" with a hiss in his lips that I knew meant I was about to get the talking to.

"You don't know what you're upset about, do you?" he asked.

"Well, I'm upset about the fact that we don't spend enough time together," I said.

"Okay, good. Here."

He took a bunch of the acting class brochures and threw them all over the fake living room I had just fake-cleaned, turned to my stage husband and pointed for him to walk out of the scene. He instructed me, "Now, you start picking those up and keep picking 'em up until you've got them all in a neat stack. But keep going through the scene as usual."

My cheeks and chest felt hot with embarrassment. It seemed so stupid to pick up these stupid brochures in our stupid fake living room, but I did until my stage husband walked back into the room, talking and chatting about his happy day while I continued to pick up these stupid pieces of paper. Now, not only were my cheeks hot, but I was actually growing angrier about the fact that my stage husband and I weren't spending enough time together. My dialogue was coming out with more venom and just as I felt myself about to get teary my teacher called, "Scene."

This is when I learned about what actors call "doing the work." Sometimes "the work" has nothing to do with the scene at hand. Those brochures would not naturally have been strewn around our fake living room, but somehow having to pick up those brochures in our fake living room produced real emotion for me, helping me to arrive at a point where I was really angry, really annoyed, really pissed off, not just pretending to do what I imagined angry people do.

This was one of the nights when I wished our acting class were followed by a therapy session, because while the next pair of classmates had their moment at our acting teacher's guillotine, I was contemplating the idea of doing the work and how it applied to my real life. A part of breaking rhythm is being willing to do the work, willing to scrub toilets to get to your dream, willing to spend quality time with God and loved ones to cultivate better relationships, willing to let God use your experiences to mature and prepare you for what's to come.

THE MOMENT BEFORE

So you've reached the end of this book, and maybe not much has changed. Unfortunately, I haven't worked out a deal where my words have magic powers to change your present circumstances or mine. We are still "here," wherever here is for you and for me. But here is a great place to practice freestyling, dancing with the One who knows better than you, making the most of those moments of quiet.

Embracing broken rhythm means accepting that there are many things in life you can't control. So maybe instead of spending your time trying to wrestle down the details of your life, now is a good time to bob your head to the rhythm you've got and create a rhyme.

We are His workmanship, created in Christ Jesus for good works, which God prepared beforehand that we should walk in them. (Ephesians 2:10 NKJV)

Workmanship in the Greek translates to the word *poema*, which is where we derive the English word *poem*. We are God's poetry. What God does in our lives has rhythm, has rhyme, and is poetry.

Following Jesus means you agree to submit to his rhythm, to give over your life, ideas, desires and future to him. I hope that in these pages you have found some solace, truth and challenge. As you leave these pages I hope you will find the inspiration and encouragement to continue the wild ride that is following Christ.

Improv has almost the same rules as fighting fair: You can't bring all these external facts that have nothing to do with the moment at hand. When you're in the scene you have to lean into it, focused on your partner and the present moment. Know the backstory, but don't let it distract you.

It's so easy to focus on the moments before, but improvisation forces you to be present where you are. And not just be present but do what you can where you are.

My acting teacher talked about the moment before: examining a character's emotions, thoughts and setting right before they enter a scene. Were the character's parents abusive? Loving? Distant? Did she feel pretty as a child? Where did he grow up? It is our tendency to get caught up in the whole backstory. But these things don't help the current scene as much. What mostly helps the scene is the immediate moment that led you here.

When I'm on stage, I have my own personal "moment before." It typically happens on the side of stage, a few minutes before I go on. In that moment, how small I am when standing next to God becomes a stark reality. I realize I don't deserve to be there. I haven't been afforded the opportunity of going on stage because I'm awesome or eloquent or grand or amazing. I've simply been afforded the opportunity because God has allowed it. I stand in his name and reputation. And that is enough. Then I think about how much God loves me. I think about how much my little brain can fathom of his love, about how much I don't deserve this either, but he lavishes, pours, gives his love anyway.

GOD, BARBARA WALTERS AND ME

God is the great improviser. The same way mountains remind some people of God's majesty, an amazing jazz riff, a kicking hip hop beat, a fresh break dance move, the lilt in a poet's pause remind me of God's creativity. He is not the most creative being, he is *The* Creative Being. To be honest, as arrogant as it sounds, sometimes I just think I'm smarter than he is. I think I've pretty much got my whole life figured out. I treat him like some absentminded parent, with my life as some permission slip he just needs to sign, endorsing whatever I've come up with.

The journalist in me often wants to interview God. Ever since I was a kid I've had a fascination with Barbara Walters. I wanted to be her, and not just because she made people cry. I don't want to make God cry, but I do want to ask him some hard-line questions. In the past I thought there would be a lot of red tape, bureaucracy and runaround to get to him. But it turns out when you call him he answers directly.

I imagine God would be quiet at first. I'd take his silence for judgment, assuming his silence meant he'd found fault with me. I'd probably start to cry, preparing myself for the ultimate diss and dismissal. Or I'd start to explain myself, justifying, confessing.

God would probably look at me the way my husband looks at me when I'm talking too much to cover how insecure I feel, the look that says, "I just love you and that doesn't need to be justified or explained away. I just want you. No façade, no masks, no makeup, you."

I think by the time I got to God, sitting down on some plush couch in a lavishly understated living room, I would discover God's not the diva that people make him out to be. I imagine that he would be beautiful, some rich color that you rarely if ever see on a human being. He would behave like a true rich person, dressing humbly and not showing much sign of how much he was really worth. He would have kind eyes, the kind of eyes that would make an interviewer feel interviewed.

I would fumble with notes, shuffle cards, turn pages, cross my legs, lean back as if I were going to throw a curve ball to the One who already knew what I was thinking.

"So you have a lot of myths to dispel, don't you?" I'd say.

He'd nod.

"Are you as uptight as people say you are?"

He'd laugh and then get really serious. So serious that for a minute I'd be a little scared for my life. Then he'd laugh again, get real serious, laugh once more and probably say, "What do you think?"

Memories the length of a commercial would pass through my mind: that last year of college when I had no idea what I was going to do with my life, the moments I'm still not sure if I'll ever be good enough. Then I'd look at him and wonder if he was really all about love like his bio said he was and if he was why he allowed so much pain.

"Let's take a walk," he'd say.

We'd do a walking tour of his estate, because that's what you do during a Barbara Walters interview. He'd have the greenest grass and the most beautiful mountains, and all the people living there with him would be so unique and different. We'd come back inside for the sweetest, coldest glass of sweet tea I'd ever had because obviously God drinks sweet tea.

I'd walk by his mantel and see pictures of a face I'd recognize, my own. Except they were pictures a camera didn't take. They were special moments God had taken note of. As he starts to reminisce on the first time I held a mic in vacation Bible school, the tears I cried when I had to move states in the middle of my sixth-grade year, the first time I heard "Under the Bridge" by the Red Hot Chili Peppers and loved rock-and-roll music, the day I found my wedding dress and for the first time in my life felt like a princess.

After I'd asked all the questions I needed for my 20/20 special,

I'd walk away as many journalists do after interviewing an artist and realize I'd never quite understand God. But maybe understanding God wasn't the point. I mean, he wouldn't be God if I could understand him. It seemed like his goal wasn't for me to understand, his goal was for me to be with him and he with me, to tune my ear and heart to his rhythm, in hopes that I'd discover being with him is enough.

Scene.

REFERENCED WORKS

Hans Christian Anderson, *Fairy Tales* (New York: Chronicle, 1992).

Bill Brewster and Frank Broughton, *Last Night a DJ Saved My Life* (New York: Grove Press, 2000).

Nicholas Evans, *The Horse Whisperer* (New York: Random House, 1995).

Tina Fey, *Bossypants* (New York: Little, Brown and Company, 2011).

Hannah Hurnard, *Hind's Feet on High Places* (East Sussex, U.K.: Gardners, 2008).

Bruce Lee and M. Uyehara, *Bruce Lee's Fighting Method* (Santa Clarita, Calif.: O'Hara Publications, Inc., 2008).

Jack London, *To Build a Fire* (Seattle: Createspace, 2009).

Sugar Ray Robinson and David Anderson, *Sugar Ray* (Cambridge, Mass.: Da Capo Press, 1994).

CONNECT WITH AMENA BROWN

web: www.amenabrown.com
email: info@amenabrown.com
Twitter: @amenabee
Facebook: /amenabrown

ACKNOWLEDGMENTS

*T*hank you to Kimberly Womble, Margaret Feinberg and Dan Kimball for continuing to (figuratively) kick me in the pants to write this book. It would not exist if it weren't for your support and friendship.

To Jayme, thanks for sharing your music with me and always hipping me to a new artist.

To Robert and Jay, although we can never seem to agree on the best rapper alive, I am thankful for all our hip hop conversations. The two of you are major reasons why I immersed myself in hip hop.

To Dave Zimmerman and the InterVarsity Press staff, thank you for believing in me and supporting me. Thank you for your patience with all my questions and changes. I appreciate you all!

To Greg Tate, you mentored me via email, coffee and a tour of Harlem. You told me the straight up truth about writing, about art, about writing about art. I am still wading through those albums, books and designers you told me to study up on. I am a better writer for having met you.

To the kind people who read these chapters and gave me honest feedback and another set of eyes: Jamila Abston, Adan Beane, Charlette Clark, Michelle Hoeft, Heath Hollensbe, Adrienne Howze, Kwajelyn Jackson, Makeda Lewis, Travis Mason, Lewis Moats, Rachel Monroe, Cole NeSmith, Vickie Owen, Kelly Pope, Lindsay Smith, Mari Wiles, Joy Worley and Brian Wurzell. All of your comments, encouragement and questions helped me to sharpen the content here. You deserve a shout out! Thank you.

To the DJs who inspire me: Opdiggy, Klever, Questlove, Jazzy Jeff and Pete Rock. Thank God for albums and what you do with them.

To Maya Angelou, Anne Lamott, Dream Hampton, Donald Miller, Toni Morrison and Tariq Trotter, your work inspires me to return to the blank page and blinking cursor.

To my dad, James Brown, for passing on his love of music to my siblings and me: Jayme, Robert and Jay. To my stepmom, Jackie Brown, for all those good choir songs you played on repeat in your car, and for teaching me harmony.

To my sister, Makeda, I'm so thankful for your art, challenge, fashion and inspiration. You keep me going in more ways than you know.

To my mom, Willa Jeanne Brown, you have believed in my writing since you stumbled on my first steno pad full of poetry. Thank you for buying me records, books and journals, and for showing me what a godly woman looks like. Your words and life example lift me up. You are a great mom and a wonderful friend. I love you.

To my Grandma Bert, I love you and all the stories I get to tell about you. Maybe one day I will fill a book with them. Thank you for all those trips to the library, for making me watch VH-1 instead of MTV when I was a kid, and for teaching me hymns while you played the piano. If it weren't for you, I would not know the Berenstain Bears, Paul Simon, Tracy Chapman or "Blessed Assurance." You are the best!

To my sweet and patient husband, Matthew "Opdiggy" Owen. I cannot count the mornings I wake up next to you and thank God that you are my husband. You are everything I prayed for and all the things I didn't know to ask God for but really needed. You inspire me, challenge me, sharpen me, love me and accept me, and God uses your love all the time to show me a glimpse of his love for me. Thank you for always believing in me, for being my husband and best friend.

Lastly, to you dear reader, thank you for checking out this book. I hope this is a spark for you to embrace and break rhythm.

SOUNDTRACK

These are some of the songs that have helped me find and break rhythm.

1. "Lessons Learned," by Alicia Keys
2. "Put Your Records On," by Corinne Bailey Rae
3. "(B Quiet Interlude)," by David Crowder Band
4. "Rebirth of Slick (Cool like Dat)," by Digable Planets
5. "That's the Way of the World," by Earth, Wind & Fire
6. "Pretty Girl," by Eric Roberson
7. "Bag Lady," by Erykah Badu
8. "A Closer Walk," by Fred Hammond
9. "The Last Time," by Gnarls Barkley
10. "You Have Me," by Gungor
11. "Strength, Courage and Wisdom," by India.Arie
12. "Tightrope," by Janelle Monae
13. "Blessed," by Jill Scott
14. "With a Little Help from My Friends," by Joe Cocker
15. "My Favorite Things," by John Coltrane
16. "I Wonder," by Kanye West
17. "Breakaway," by Kelly Clarkson
18. "Anonymous," by Kelly Love Jones
19. "Off the Wall," by Michael Jackson
20. "So What," by Miles Davis
21. "Liberation," by Outkast
22. "Under the Bridge," by the Red Hot Chili Peppers
23. "Dear God 2.0," by The Roots
24. "Get By," by Talib Kweli
25. "My Heart, Your Home," by Watermark

IVP *Crescendo*
COURAGE. CONFIDENCE. CALLING.

Some voices challenge us. Others support or encourage us. Voices can move us to change our minds, draw close to God, discover a new spiritual gift. The voices of others are shaping who we are.

The voices behind IVP Crescendo join together to draw us into God's story. We'll discover God's work around the globe even as we learn to love the people around the corner. We'll have opportunity to heal our places of pain. We'll discover new ways to love our families. We'll hear God's voice speaking into our lives as we discover new places of influence.

IVP Crescendo invites you to join in the rising chorus

- *to listen to the voices of others*
- *to hear the voice of God*
- *and to grow your own voice in*

COURAGE. CONFIDENCE. CALLING.

Stay in touch with IVP Crescendo:
ivpress.com/crescendo-social